PETER B. KENEN   *Columbia University*

International
Economics.

SECOND EDITION

PRENTICE-HALL, INC.   *Englewood Cliffs, New Jersey*

HF
1411
.K4
1967

PRENTICE-HALL FOUNDATIONS
OF MODERN ECONOMICS SERIES

Otto Eckstein, *Editor*

Current printing (last digit):
10 9 8 7 6 5 4 3 2 1

PRENTICE-HALL INTERNATIONAL INC., *London*
PRENTICE-HALL OF AUSTRALIA, PTY., LTD., *Sydney*
PRENTICE-HALL OF CANADA, LTD., *Toronto*
PRENTICE-HALL OF INDIA PVT. LTD., *New Delhi*
PRENTICE-HALL OF JAPAN, INC., *Tokyo*

Foundations

of Modern Economics Series

Economics has grown so rapidly in recent years, it has increased so much in scope and depth, and the new dominance of the empirical approach has so transformed its character, that no one book can do it justice today. To fill this need, the Foundations of Modern Economics Series was conceived. The Series, brief books written by leading specialists, reflects the structure, content, and key scientific and policy issues of each field. Used in combination, the Series provides the material for the basic one-year college course. The analytical core of economics is presented in *Prices and Markets* and *National Income Analysis,* which are basic to the various fields of application. *Prices and Markets,* a new book prepared especially for this edition of the Series, takes the beginning student through the elements of that subject step-by-step. *The Price System* is a more sophisticated alternative carried over from the first edition. Two books in the Series, *The Evolution of Modern Economics* and *Economic Development: Past and Present,* can be read without prerequisite and can serve as an introduction to the subject.

The Foundations approach enables an instructor to devise his own course curriculum rather than to follow the format of the traditional textbook. Once analytical principles have been mastered, many sequences of topics can be arranged and specific areas can be explored at length. An instructor not interested in a complete survey course can omit some books and concentrate on a detailed study of a few fields. One-semester courses stressing either macro-

v

or micro-economics can be readily devised. The instructors guide to the Series indicates the variety of ways the books in the Series can be used.

This Series is an experiment in teaching. The positive response to the first edition has encouraged us to continue, and to develop and improve, the approach. The thoughtful reactions of many teachers who have used the books in the past have been of immense help in preparing the second edition —in improving the integration of the Series, in smoothing some rough spots in exposition, and in suggesting additional topics for coverage.

The books do not offer settled conclusions. They introduce the central problems of each field and indicate how economic analysis enables the reader to think more intelligently about them, to make him a more thoughtful citizen, and to encourage him to pursue the subject further.

Otto Eckstein, *Editor*

Contents

International Economics

The Nation

as an Economic Unit

CHAPTER ONE

FOREIGN AND DOMESTIC TRANSACTIONS

The study of foreign trade and finance is among the oldest specialties within economic inquiry. It was conceived in the sixteenth century, a lusty child of Europe's passion for Spanish gold, and grew to maturity in the turbulent years that witnessed the articulation of modern nation-states. In the eighteenth and nineteenth centuries it attracted the very best economists, including Adam Smith, David Ricardo, and John Stuart Mill, whose work supplied the legacy of insights and concepts that have endured to guide the economists of even our own era. (It is interesting to note that Mill furnished the first full formulation of the "law of supply and demand" while trying to explain price determination in international markets, and that, similarly, a large part of modern monetary theory emerged from early efforts to show how foreign trade can affect the level of domestic prices.)

International economics flourishes today because the facts and problems that brought it into being still compel our urgent attention. First, economic conditions and institutions are more uniform within countries. Second, foreign transactions are specially encumbered by public policy. These two points are easy to illustrate.

Language, law, and custom rarely differ much within a single country. This internal uniformity makes for easy movement of labor, capital, and enterprise. The tax system is also homogeneous within a country, but differs very markedly from one country to

1

the next. True, the tax systems of our 50 separate states differ quite widely. But federal tax rates are higher than state rates, and you may deduct state tax payments from your gross income when you calculate your federal income-tax. The national tax system thereby helps to average out regional differences. Furthermore, federal spending tends increasingly to overlay local variations in the quality and quantity of public services.

Internal monetary differences are smallest of all. An elaborate network of markets connects financial institutions within the United States. Funds can flow from region to region, and borrowers can raise cash where it is cheapest, whittling down regional differences in credit conditions. Finally and most important, a single currency is used throughout the country. A five-dollar bill issued by the Federal Reserve Bank of Richmond circulates freely across the United States; it must be accepted everywhere. For that matter, you can cash a check wherever you are known, even if you write the check on a bank hundreds of miles away. How much more complicated life would be if merchants refused to accept currency or checks from other Federal Reserve Districts! You would have to scan every dollar bill, weed out those from other Districts, and swap them for local money at your bank; you would also have to carry a large quantity of cash while traveling and would have to trade one kind for another when crossing state lines.

Goods flow freely among our 50 states. In fact, the American Constitution expressly forbids local interference with interstate commerce. The authors of the Constitution believed that free trade among the states would help cement their fragile political union. For similar reasons France, Italy, Germany, the Netherlands, Belgium, and Luxembourg are currently forging a Common Market in Western Europe as the first step toward a political confederation; they will soon permit a free flow of goods inside Western Europe and will impose a common tariff on goods from outside. But trade between countries is ordinarily burdened with customs tariffs that work to raise the prices of imported goods; and countries have sometimes used more formidable barriers—quotas that restrict the quantity of imports or the freedom to buy foreign currency. The United States puts quotas on foreign petroleum and on each of a dozen farm products. The quotas on imported oil protect the domestic oil industry; those on farm products are meant to deny foreign farmers the benefits provided by our high price supports for farm products. These tariffs and quantitative barriers are doubly restrictive. First, they raise the prices of foreign goods and handicap those goods in competition with domestic products. Second, they impose a heavy workload on the would-be importer. Look at the fragment from the U.S. tariff schedule reproduced in Fig. 1-1, and try to compute the rate of duty on a shockproof, self-winding watch, 1 inch wide, with 16 jewels.

Differences between monetary systems may have an even greater adverse impact on foreign trade than tariffs and quotas. Almost all international transactions involve two or more moneys. An American wholesaler importing

PARA. 367(a)(1-5): Watches and watch movements, and timekeeping, measuring or indicating mechanisms, devices, and instruments, whether or not designed to be worn or carried on or about the person, less than 1 77/100 inches wide, whether or not in cases, etc., with or without dials.

Having more than 15, but not more than 17 jewels:		
More than 1½, less than 1 77/100 inches wide	$1.25	ea.
More than 1 2/10, not more than 1½ inches wide	1.35	ea.
More than 1, not more than 1 2/10 inches wide	1.35	ea.
More than 9/10, not more than 1 inch wide	1.75	ea.
More than 8/10, not more than 9/10 inches wide	2.00	ea.
More than 6/10, not more than 8/10 inches wide	2.02½	ea.
6/10 inches, or less wide	2.50	ea.
Adjustments and jewels in movements having more than 15, but not more than 12 jewels:		
Adjustments (adjustment to temperature equals 2 adjustments)	.50	ea. add'l
Jewels	.13½	ea. add'l
Movements operating in excess of 47 hours without rewinding or if self-winding	.75	ea. add'l

FIG. 1-1 A fragment of the U.S. tariff schedule. The tariff on a single watch must be calculated by adding up several separate rates: the basic rate (based on width and jewels), the extra duty on adjustments, the duty on each jewel, and the special duty on self-winding mechanisms.

French champagne has first to determine its price in French francs, then the price of the franc in U.S. dollars—the franc-dollar *exchange rate.* He must order the champagne, buy French francs with dollars, then pay over the francs to the French exporter. He thereby incurs extra cost and runs extra risks. The costs are the commissions charged by specialized dealers in foreign exchange. The risks arise because exchange rates can change. Most governments are pledged to maintain their exchange rates at or near fixed points called *parities.* Currently, for example, you can buy a French franc for 20¼ cents, or 4.94 French francs for a dollar. But governments allow exchange rates to change by as much as 2 per cent of parity in response to variations in supply and demand, and sometimes make changes in the parities themselves. In 1956 the French franc was *devalued* (made cheaper in terms of other currencies), going from 3.50 for a dollar to 4.20 for a dollar; and in 1958 it was devalued again, this time from 4.20 to 4.94 per dollar. In 1961, by contrast, the German mark and Dutch guilder were made to *appreciate* (made more expensive in terms of other currencies). Day-to-day changes in exchange rates can cut into traders' profits, and sudden changes in the parities can turn profits into losses. The American importer of French champagne could lose heavily if the price of the franc were to rise on the foreign-exchange market after he had signed his sales contract but before he had bought his francs.[1]

[1] Traders and investors can sometimes protect themselves against exchange-rate changes by buying or selling foreign currency on the *forward* foreign-exchange market. There, they can arrange to swap dollars for francs three months from now, at a price (exchange rate) fixed today. Doing so, however, they merely transform risk into cost, for forward foreign exchange may be more expensive than *spot* (current) foreign exchange.

Foreign investors have also to cope with foreign-exchange problems, and these may be more complex than those faced by traders, for investors have a longer time-horizon. They likewise face difficult tax problems, as tax laws and tax rates differ radically from one country to the next.

PERSPECTIVES AND CRITERIA

The international economist views the world as a community of separate nations, each with its own constellation of natural resources, capital, knowledge, and manpower, its own social and economic institutions, and its own economic policies. He usually assumes that transport costs are negligible and that most markets are purely competitive. He often assumes that labor and capital are perfectly mobile within each country, but not free to move from one country to the next.

Using these assumptions, he seeks to explain international flows of goods, services, and capital, to assess their impact on domestic welfare, and to forecast their response to changes in national policies. He concentrates on policies expressly designed to affect foreign trade and payments—those involving tariffs, exchange rates, and the taxation of foreign-source income. But he must also look at other policies—at tax rates, public spending, monetary management, labor legislation, and the rest—since they prescribe the terms on which international transactions take place.

The international economist will sometimes study trade and payments from the standpoint of a single country, but is just as likely to adopt a cosmopolitan perspective and seek to ascertain their impact on the world as a whole. When taking a single country's viewpoint, he is apt to begin his analysis by pretending that the country in question was at first isolated from the outside world, but then began to trade with other countries. When taking the cosmopolitan viewpoint, he is likely to start out by pretending that there were at first no differences in policies or barriers to trade among its several regions, but that those regions then became separate nations, each with its own institutions and policies. The perspectives and assumptions he employs in his analysis may greatly affect his conclusions, especially those that pertain to the selection of national policies.

Whatever his particular perspective, however, the international economist is chiefly concerned with individuals. Like other economists, he is an intellectual descendant of Adam Smith and of the nineteenth-century Utilitarians, and though he may for analytical purposes treat the nation as a single unit, he is not likely to regard it as the end in view. Instead, he appraises any change in public policy by the same criteria his confrères employ in other specialities. He says that such a change is good if those individuals who gain by the change could compensate those who lose. Furthermore, he uses the same tests of economic performance that guide other specialists.

First, he is concerned with *efficiency:* How do international trade and payments affect the allocation of resources within a country? How do they redistribute economic tasks among the participating countries?

Second, he is concerned with *equity:* How does trade alter the distribution of income and wealth within a country? How does it redistribute income and wealth among countries?

Third, he is concerned with *stability:* How does trade affect a country's reaction to domestic disturbances and its freedom to deal with domestic problems? Does it, perhaps, "import" extra instability through its external transactions?

Fourth, he is concerned with *economic growth:* Does a country's foreign trade affect its growth rate? Should the less-developed countries gear their new production to foreign markets, making their way as exporters, or should they draw back from foreign trade to seek greater self-sufficiency?

Do not be deceived by the abstract formulation of these questions. The search for answers is propelled by the daily needs of business and government, not by scientific curiosity alone. The problems posed by foreign trade, investment, and aid, and by international monetary relations, impinge on a host of issues confronting the United States. After a century of intensive exploitation, its endowment of raw materials is dwindling. Should it cut back its domestic output of ores and oil to rely instead on cheaper foreign sources, or should it protect its domestic producers against import competition to encourage further exploration and exploitation? How can the United States act to improve the distribution of the world's food supplies? Can it reconcile its own farm policies with those of other exporting countries like Canada and, simultaneously, with those of key importers like Britain and India? Should our tax policies be changed in response to the surge of private American investment abroad—the building of factories in Europe to manufacture goods that were formerly exported from the United States? How will this migration of capital and enterprise affect economic life here and abroad?

How can the United States maintain an over-all balance in its international transactions, given its commitments to foster economic growth at home and also to defend and develop friendly foreign countries? Is the special role of the U.S. dollar as an international currency beneficial, or burdensome? If beneficial, how can it be strengthened? If burdensome, how can the international monetary system be altered without damaging the network of trade and payments built up so patiently since the Second World War? How best can the United States and other countries aid the new nations of Asia, Africa, and Latin America, and how will these young countries fit into world trade once they have begun to modernize their own economies?

We shall not try to survey this whole range of issues in the hundred pages at our disposal, but will try to illustrate the methods and perspectives employed by economists as *they* seek to answer them. In Chapters 2 and 3 we **5** will ask how international trade and investment affect the allocation of world resources, and how the various barriers modify that allocation; we will glance at the diplomacy of tariff policy; and we will take a quick tour of the European Common Market. In Chapters 4 and 5 we will take up the *balance of payments* and the foreign-exchange market; we will study equilibrium, displacement, and adjustment in international payments; and we will survey the roles of gold and the U.S. dollar in the international monetary system. Finally, in Chapter 6, we will examine foreign trade and investment as "engines" of economic growth, seeking to determine how they can contribute to the development of the new nations.

Trade

and Resource Allocation

CHAPTER TWO

THE BASIS FOR TRADE
AND GAINS FROM TRADE

Differences in prices are the basic cause of trade and reflect international differences in costs. But why should costs differ from country to country? How can Japan produce cameras, sewing machines, and cotton shirts more cheaply than the United States? Many people would reply that Japan has lower costs because it has lower wages, and wages are important costs. This explanation seems plausible enough; it is firmly based on fact. But it is not adequate.

If wage rates were decisive for cost differences and trade, Japan would undersell the United States in every product line and every market. Yet Japan imports machinery and cotton from the United States, and other low-wage countries buy American goods in great variety and enormous quantities. As a matter of fact, the United States sells more to other countries than it buys abroad, despite its high wages. Differences in wage rates, then, cannot explain trade patterns, and one must look elsewhere for the basis of trade.

An enduring two-way flow of goods must be traced to systematic international differences in the *structure* of costs and prices: some things must be cheaper to produce at home and will be exported to other countries; some things must be cheaper to produce abroad and will be imported from other countries. This generaliza-

7

tion is basic to the theory of foreign trade, and is known as the *principle of comparative advantage*. Stated most precisely, it asserts that a country will export the products which it can produce at the lowest *relative* cost. Japan, it contends, can export cameras and textiles because it can produce those goods with the least sacrifice of alternative production. The United States can export machinery and cotton because it can produce those goods with the smallest sacrifice. Cameras may be cheaper than machines in both countries, but the cost difference is far from uniform, thus creating opportunities for profitable trade.

The Sources of Comparative Advantage

A nation's comparative advantage and trade pattern are heavily affected by its resource endowment—both natural and man-made. Nature has decreed important and enduring differences between countries. Some of them are rich in copper, others in petroleum; some have huge waterfalls, others have fertile plains. Some countries have just enough rainfall for rice or cotton cultivation, while some have too much, and others have next to none. Furthermore, some countries have the resource *combinations* required for the performance of certain vital tasks: one may have the plains *and* rainfall needed to grow wheat; another may have a rich deposit of iron ore *next to* a waterway that can carry ore to coal. Finally, some countries have populations large enough to man and support great, complex industries, but others are so very underpopulated that their land cannot even be worked or their ores extracted.

In one sense, people are a natural resource; in another, they are a major man-made resource. Mere numbers are the gift of nature. But the skills and attitudes of a population are the work of man and strongly influence a country's comparative advantage. A nation rich in people but poor in skills may be suited to certain tasks, but not to the production and export of manufactured goods. A nation that has very few persons per square mile but has lavished its energies on technical training is likely to enjoy a comparative advantage in the production of precision goods.

Going one step further, we must distinguish between types of skill. Some nations have large numbers of factory workers adept at handling modern machinery. Others have an abundance of engineers and scientists and specialize in new, research-laden products. It has been said, for example, that the United States enjoys a comparative advantage in research and innovation, but that it loses out to its competitors as each of its new products ages, the market for it grows, and the knowledge required to manufacture it is diffused among other countries. The United States, it is argued, has always to race ahead in technology merely to stand still in world markets.

One part of a nation's capital stock is embodied in its labor force as agricultural, industrial, and scientific skill. Another part is embodied in physical equipment: roads, airports, harbors, and dams; trucks, aircraft, ships, and turbines; factories and office buildings; tractors, lathes, conveyers, and type-

8

writers. These represent the portion of past output that was reserved for investment rather than consumption.

Notice that natural and man-made resources can interact powerfully. Bauxite was not valued as a natural resource until the development of the electrolytic process for extracting aluminum, and of the cheap electric power required to fuel that process. Aluminum itself was not very valuable until the metalworking industries found ways to use it. Pitchblende was a geological curiosity until man's skill and malevolence found a use for uranium, and ways to separate one isotope from others. Population also interacts with technology. Modern mass-production methods need mass markets and are apt to take root first in regions of dense settlement that provide outlets for large lots of standardized products. In consequence, such regions are apt to enjoy a comparative advantage in the export of mass-produced articles, and they may well retain their advantage *vis-à-vis* regions that start later or on a smaller scale. Notice, too, that comparative advantage always has a time dimension. It depends on the state of technology at a given moment and on its subsequent diffusion. It also depends on the history of capital accumulation and, therefore, on the rate of economic growth.

A Simple Model

To show how a difference in resource endowments can call forth foreign trade, consider two countries, America and Britain, which are identical in all ways but one. Both of them have 120 man-days of labor available. Both use 2 man-days of labor to grow a ton of potatoes and have enough arable land to employ all their workers in potato-farming. But America's coal deposits are very near to the surface and only 1 man-day of labor is required to dig out a ton, while Britain's deposits are much farther down and 4 man-days of labor are required to dig out a ton. If its whole labor force were employed growing potatoes, America could produce 60 tons per day; 2 man-days of labor can grow a single ton and 120 man-days of labor are available. If, instead, the whole labor force were employed digging coal, America could produce 120 tons per day; 1 man-day of labor can dig out a single ton and 120 man-days are available. If, finally, America wished to produce some potatoes and some coal, it could secure any one of several combinations. To produce a single ton of coal, it would have to divert 1 man-day of labor from its potato fields, reducing potato output by half a ton. To produce 2 tons of coal, it would have to divert 2 man-days from the potato fields, reducing potato output by 1 ton.

America's *production possibilities* are summarized by the line AB in Fig. 2-1. The distance OA measures the output of coal that would be obtained if the entire labor force worked in the coal mines (120 tons); the distance OB measures the output of potatoes that would be obtained if the entire labor force worked in the potato fields (60 tons). Points along the line AB describe the combinations of coal and potatoes that could be produced simultaneously.

9

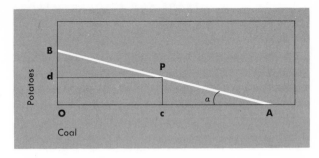

FIG. 2-1 American production possibilities. The line AB shows how many tons of potatoes America can grow for a given level of coal production. If America produced Oc tons of coal, it could grow Od tons of potatoes. The steepness of AB (measured by angle a) gives the price of coal in terms of potatoes.

At point *P*, for example, America would be producing *Oc* coal and *Od* potatoes. It would obtain *Oc* coal by foregoing *Bd* potatoes.

If Americans were not allowed to trade with outsiders, their pattern of consumption would have to coincide with one of the coal and potato combinations lying on *AB*. The output mix prevailing at a particular time would, of course, depend on consumer preferences—demand conditions—and on the price of coal in terms of potatoes. That price ratio, in turn, would be given by the comparative labor costs of coal and potato production. Labor is the only variable input (factor of production) used in this very simple economy, and a single man-day of labor can mine a whole ton of coal but can only grow half a ton of potatoes. A ton of coal will therefore cost a single man-day's wage, while a ton of potatoes will cost 2 man-days' wages. A ton of coal will be half as expensive as a ton of potatoes, and it will exchange for half a ton of potatoes in America's markets.[1] This same price relationship appears in Fig. 2-1; it is represented by the slope (steepness) of *AB*, the production possibilities frontier. The distance *OB* is half the distance *OA*, indicating that a ton of coal will sell for half a ton of potatoes.

Britain also needs 2 man-days of labor to produce a ton of potatoes, and consequently could grow 60 tons if it used all its labor in its potato patches. But it needs 4 man-days of labor to dig out a ton of coal, and could mine only 30 tons if it used all its labor in its coal mines. By implication, Britain could produce a single ton of coal by diverting 4 man-days of labor from potato-growing, thereby giving up 2 tons of potatoes. Britain's production possibilities are described by the line *A'B'* in Fig. 2-2. Maximum potato

---

[1] One can arrive at this same result by examining *marginal* costs. If product markets are perfectly competitive, prices must equal marginal costs. If labor is the only variable input and labor requirements are constant for all output levels, marginal costs must equal labor requirements per unit of extra output multiplied by the wage rate. Hence:

Price of Coal = Marginal Cost of Coal = Wage Rate × Man-days of Labor Needed to Produce a Ton of Coal

Price of Potatoes = Marginal Cost of Potatoes = Wage Rate × Man-days of Labor Needed to Produce a Ton of Potatoes

Therefore:

$$\frac{\text{Price of Coal}}{\text{Price of Potatoes}} = \frac{\text{Man-days Needed to Produce a Ton of Coal}}{\text{Man-days Needed to Produce a Ton of Potatoes}}$$

The wage rate cancels out in this calculation, for it must be the same in both industries.

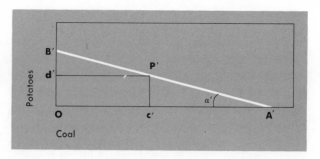

FIG. 2-2 British production possibilities. The $A'B'$ shows how many tons of potatoes Britain can grow for a given level of coal production. The steepness of $A'B'$ (measured by angle a') gives the price of coal in terms of potatoes. Britain can produce as many potatoes as America (OB' equals OB in Fig. 2-1), but far less coal.

output, OB', is the same as in America, because the two countries are endowed with the same amounts of labor and are equally efficient in potato-growing. But maximum coal output, OA', is smaller in Britain than in America, for Britain's coal lies somewhat deeper in the ground.

The line $A'B'$ in Fig. 2-2 is much steeper than the line AB in Fig. 2-1. This difference is explained by the difference in mining costs and implies a difference in relative prices. British coal must be twice as expensive as British potatoes, for labor costs are twice as high. Isolated from the outside world, Britain would produce and consume some combination of coal and potatoes lying on $A'B'$, and a ton of coal would be worth 2 tons of potatoes.

But now allow America and Britain to trade and suppose that goods can move between them without transport costs. The opportunity for trade will create a single Anglo-American market and, therefore, a single price for coal in terms of potatoes. This new common price will lie between the national extremes—less than the prior British price (2 tons of potatoes per ton of coal) and higher than the prior American price (half a ton of potatoes per ton of coal).[2] Britain can now obtain a ton of coal without surrendering as many potatoes as it had to sacrifice to furnish its own coal. It will tend to specialize in potato-growing and will use its potatoes to buy American coal. America is able to obtain more potatoes for its coal. It will tend to specialize in coal-mining and to use its coal to buy British potatoes.

To illustrate this rearrangement of production, suppose that the new Anglo-American coal price is stabilized at 1 ton of potatoes per ton of coal. Britain can now import a ton of coal by growing and exporting a single ton of potatoes. Without trade, by contrast, it had to sacrifice 2 tons of potatoes to produce a ton of coal. In effect, Britain saves 2 man-days of labor on each ton of coal consumed. For its part, America can import a ton of potatoes by mining and exporting a single ton of coal. Without trade, it had to sacrifice 2

---

[2] The new common price for coal could also settle at one of the national extremes. In that case, one country would capture all the gains from trade, but the other would be no worse off than it was without trade. If the price came to rest at the old British level, America would garner all the gains from trade; it would get its potatoes cheaper than it could at home. If the price came to rest at the old American level, Britain would garner all the gains from trade; it would get its coal cheaper than it could at home. The determination of the actual price ratio and of the consumption point, Q in Fig. 2-3, will depend upon demand conditions in the two countries.

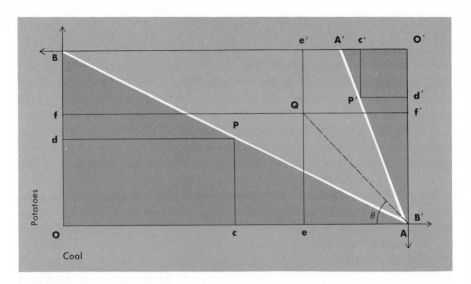

FIG. 2-3 Trade between America and Britain. Before trade, America produced Oc coal and Od potatoes. Britain produced O'c' coal and O'd' potatoes, and each country consumed all it produced. When trade is opened, America produces OA coal and no potatoes; Britain produces O'B' potatoes and no coal. America consumes Oe coal and exports eA coal to buy British potatoes; Britain consumes O'f' pototoes and exports f'B' potatoes to buy American coal. America can then consume Of potatoes (Of being equal to f'B' British exports); Britain can consume O'e' coal (O'e' being equal to eA American exports). Each country can consume more of both products than it did before trade. The price of coal, shown by the θ, is higher than the pretrade British price (the slope of A'B').

tons of coal to produce a ton of potatoes. America saves 1 man-day of labor on each ton of potatoes consumed.

Figure 2-3 restates these results with greater generality. There, the left-hand triangle, OAB, is the American production-possibilities frontier, just as it appeared in Fig. 2-1. The right-hand triangle $O'A'B'$ is Britain's production-possibilities frontier, taken from Fig. 2-2 but flipped upside-down. If America and Britain could not trade, each would be confined to its own frontier, America at P and Britain at P'. When they are allowed to trade, they can rearrange production and consumption to mutual advantage. America can specialize in coal-mining, using all its labor to produce OA tons. Britain can specialize in potato-farming, using all its labor to produce $O'B'$ tons. America can then consume Oe tons of coal and export eA tons to pay for potatoes. Britain can consume $O'f'$ tons of potatoes and export $f'B'$ tons to pay for coal. America can buy Of tons of potatoes (equal to the $f'B'$ Britain will export), and Britain can buy $O'e'$ tons of coal (equal to the eA tons America will export). American consumption can move from P to Q, and British consumption can move from P' to Q. Each country can consume more of both goods than it did before trade.[3]

Figure 2-3 describes two ways to view the gains from trade. First, it

[3] The situation described in Fig. 2-3 is not the only possibility. The point Q could settle down anywhere within the unshaded part of the diagram, depending on demand

shows that every country can escape the confines of its own resource endowment. Before trade, each country had to consume a combination of coal and potatoes lying on its own production-possibilities frontier. Its choice was restricted by its resource endowment. But trade allows every country to reshuffle output and to consume a combination of commodities it could never produce by itself. In consequence, the individual consumer enjoys a wider range of choice. Figure 2-3 also shows that trade enlarges global output by allowing every country to specialize in those tasks it does best. Before trade, total coal output was Oc plus $c'O'$. With trade, it rises to OA (an increase of ce plus $e'c'$). Before trade, total potato output was Od plus $d'O'$. With trade, it rises to $O'B'$ (an increase of df plus $f'd'$). This increase in output was required for each country to increase its consumption of both commodities in the fashion described by Fig. 2-3. It also leads to a basic proposition in international economics: *Free trade is the best regime for the world as a whole.* The increase in coal and potato output shown by Fig. 2-3 is the largest increase possible. Hence, free trade allocates economic tasks to maximize world output and income.

Productivity, Wages, and Prices

Figure 2-3 describes the free-trade price of coal as the slope (steepness) of the dotted line AQ. This line is steeper than AB, but flatter than $A'B'$. Coal has become more expensive in America, but cheaper than it was in Britain. But we have not been shown how this price comes into being. To study this important process, we must take a look at wage rates, prices, and exchange rates.

Suppose that the American wage rate stands at $15 per man-day, while the British wage rate stands at £5. At the opening of trade, a ton of American potatoes will cost $30 (2 man-days are needed to grow a ton), and a ton of coal will cost $15 (1 man-day is needed to mine a ton). A ton of British potatoes will cost £10 (2 man-days are needed to grow a ton), and a ton of coal will cost £20 (4 man-days are needed to mine a ton).

Suppose, further, that the exchange rate between the dollar and the pound has been fixed by international agreement at $3 per pound. The dollar price of British potatoes will be $30 per ton; the dollar price of British coal will be $60 per ton. Neither country will have reason to import potatoes, for the dollar prices are the same. But Britain will import American coal, since British coal costs $60 a ton while American coal costs $15 a ton.

If both countries' workers were fully employed before trade began, the

---

conditions. Furthermore, Q could come to rest on AB or $A'B'$, the extreme cases mentioned in the previous footnote. If Q came to rest on AB, Britain would specialize completely and take all the gains from trade. America would tend to specialize in coal, but would also grow potatoes. If Q came to rest on $A'B'$, America would specialize completely and take all the gains from trade. Britain would tend to specialize in potatoes, but would also mine coal.

advent of trade will cause an excess demand for labor in America because of the British demand for American coal. It will also cause unemployment in Britain because of the shift in British demand from domestic to foreign coal. In consequence, wage rates will rise in America and fall in Britain. This change in wages, however, will make British potatoes cheaper than American, whether priced in dollars or pounds, and both countries' consumers will start to buy potatoes in Britain. British farmers will plant larger crops, taking up the labor released from Britain's coal mines; American farmers will cut back their crops, releasing labor to America's mines.

This process will not cease until unemployment disappears in the British coal mines and the labor shortage ends in America's coal mines. And these things will not happen until consumers rearrange their purchases in response to the price changes resulting from the wage-rate change. When, finally, those wage changes have ceased, the price of American coal will be higher than it was to start (because of the increase in American wages), while the price of British potatoes will be lower than it was to start (because of the decrease in British wages). The wage-rate changes will have offset America's higher productivity, allowing Britain's comparative advantage in potato-growing to show through as a lower price.[4]

Some Evidence

Statistical studies of trade and productivity show that the principle of comparative advantage can explain actual patterns of trade, despite the existence of tariffs and other trade barriers. Differences in wage rates serve to offset over-all differences in national efficiency. Trade flows are consequently governed by differences in relative internal costs, reflecting variations in comparative efficiency from one domestic industry to the next.

A British economist, Sir Donald MacDougall, has compared British and American exports prior to the Second World War, looking at 24 separate industries. His results are summarized in Section A of Table 2-1. In every case, American output per worker was higher than British output per worker. But it was 5.4 times as high in the production of electric-light bulbs and only 1.1 times as high in the production of cement. Average American wage rates, by contrast, were about twice as high as average British wage rates. Whenever, then, British workers were more than half as efficient as their American competitors, British goods could compete with American goods in world markets; British exports were larger than American exports. When,

---

[4] This same process of adjustment could have been accomplished by changing the exchange rate. Suppose that money wage rates were absolutely rigid in Britain and America but that the exchange rate connecting their currencies was free to fluctuate in response to changes in supply and demand. The British demand for American coal would then be manifest in a demand for American dollars that would drive up the price of the dollar expressed in terms of pounds. This increase in the price of the dollar would lower the cost of British potatoes expressed in dollars and would raise the cost of American coal expressed in pounds. Americans would start to buy British potatoes.

instead, British productivity was less than half as high as American, the corresponding U.S. industry had the cost advantage, and in 7 out of 12 such cases, American exports were larger than British exports.

These results show up again in the post-war period. An American economist, Robert Stern, has reworked MacDougall's example using trade and labor data for 1950. At that time, U.S. wage rates were about three times as high as British wage rates. When U.S. labor productivity was more than three times British productivity, then, American exports were usually larger than British exports. Stern has also studied a larger sample comprising 39 manufacturing industries. In 15 of these 39 cases, U.S. labor was more than three times as efficient as British labor, offsetting the British wage-rate advantage, and in 11 of these 15 cases, U.S. exports were larger than British exports. In the other 24 cases, U.S. productivity was higher than British, but not as much as three times as high. In 21 of these 24 cases, British exports were larger than American exports. Stern's results are summarized in Table 2-1. Section B gives 1950 data for the same 24 industries studied by MacDougall; Section C gives 1950 data for Stern's larger sample.

Table 2-1   OUTPUT PER WORKER AND TRANSATLANTIC EXPORTS, GREAT BRITAIN AND THE UNITED STATES

		Number of Industries	
Difference in Labor Productivity	Total	In Which U.S. Exports Larger than British	In Which U.S. Exports Smaller than British
A. Pre-war trade (24 industries): U.S. wages double British wages			
U.S. output per worker more than double British	12	7	5
U.S. output per worker not more than double British	12	0	12
B. Post-war trade (24 industries): U.S. wages treble British wages			
U.S. output per worker more than treble British	7	5	2
U.S. output per worker not more than treble British	17	2	15
C. Post-war trade (39 industries): U.S. wages treble British wages			
U.S. output per worker more than treble British	15	11	4
U.S. output per worker not more than treble British	24	3	21

Source: Robert M. Stern, "British and American Productivity and Comparative Costs in International Trade," Oxford Economic Papers, Vol. 14, No. 3 (October, 1962), pp. 278, 288.

These uniformities are striking indeed. The number of exceptions is very small, especially in Stern's 39-industry sample. One would, in fact, expect many more exceptions. Most countries impose barriers to foreign trade that interfere with the principle of comparative advantage. Furthermore, each of the product classes studied includes a great number of separate commodities, and one must allow for differences in quality. Finally, labor is not the only factor of production, so that labor productivity is not the only cause of trade. If high U.S. output per worker were entirely due to the more intensive use of machinery, the U.S. advantage in efficiency would be partly offset by higher payments for the use and maintenance of that machinery.

The two-country, two-product, labor-cost model used thus far in this chapter is much like the model developed by Ricardo early in the nineteenth century. Multi-country, multi-commodity versions of that model came into use toward the end of the century and were employed to show that the chief conclusions drawn from Ricardo's work are readily susceptible of generalization. They also supplied a framework for statistical studies of the type conducted by MacDougall, Stern, and others. This family of labor-cost models can serve a great number of important purposes—to identify the gains from foreign trade and to describe the cost-price adjustments required to capture the gains from trade through international specialization. But labor-cost models shed much less light on several other aspects of foreign trade: the influence of differences in factor supplies on international specialization, the impact of economic growth on trade patterns, and the impact of trade on national economies. To study these additional issues, we require more elaborate theoretical models incorporating several factors of production: land, labor, and capital.

The multi-factor model we shall use derives from the work of two Swedish economists, Eli Heckscher and Bertil Ohlin. Like the labor-cost model you have already encountered, it excludes economies of scale, takes no account of transport costs, and assumes that tastes are the same everywhere. But unlike the labor-cost model, it goes on to assume that each country has access to the same technology, and would employ the same methods of production if confronted with identical factor prices. It thereby rules out the differences in relative efficiency that served as the basis for foreign trade in the labor-cost model we studied before.

The Heckscher-Ohlin or *factor-endowments* approach to trade theory proceeds from two suppositions:

1. Products differ in factor requirements—cars require more machine-time (capital) per worker than, say, cotton cloth or furniture, and aircraft require more machine-time than either cars or cotton cloth.[5]
2. Countries differ in factor endowments—some have large amounts of capital per worker (the capital-abundant countries) and some have very little (the labor-abundant countries).

[5] One could, of course, make cars by several methods, differing in capital-intensities. One could use a small machine-shop or an automated plant. One could also weave cloth by many methods, some of them quite highly mechanized. The choice of technique will depend on the prices of the factors of production—the wage rates paid to workers and the rental prices of machinery (the interest costs of capital and allowances for repair and depreciation). But the factor-endowments model assumes that the product which is most capital-intensive at one set of factor prices is also most capital-intensive at every other set.

The theory then argues that capital-abundant countries will tend to specialize in capital-intensive goods like cars and aircraft, and will export some of their specialties in order to import labor-intensive goods. Similarly, labor-abundant countries will specialize in labor-intensive goods and will export their own specialties in order to import capital-intensive goods. To put the proposition in general terms: *Trade will be based on differences in factor endowments and will serve to relieve each country's factor shortages.*

A numerical example will illustrate this proposition. Suppose that the production of a thousand cars requires the employment of 90 machines and 300 man-years of labor, while the production of a million yards of cloth requires the employment of 30 machines and 600 man-years of labor. If a country's entire stock of machinery and its whole labor force are used in these two industries, one can assert that:

$$\text{Machines in Use} = 90 \times \text{Thousand Cars} + 30 \times \text{Million Yards of Cloth}$$
$$\text{Labor Employed} = 300 \times \text{Thousand Cars} + 600 \times \text{Million Yards of Cloth}$$

If, next, we know how much machinery and labor is on hand, we can solve these two identities as simultaneous equations, and can thereby obtain a country's full-employment car-and-cloth combination. Consider two countries —a labor-abundant country called Manymen, and a capital-abundant country called Fewmen—with the fixed endowments of machinery and labor shown in Table 2-2. Replacing "machines in use" and "labor employed" with Manymen's stock of capital (600 machines) and labor supply (6,000 man-years), then solving for cars and cloth, we ascertain that Manymen can produce 4,000 cars and 8,000,000 yards of cloth. Repeating this procedure with Fewmen's endowment, we ascertain that Fewmen can produce 9,000 cars and 3,000,000 yards of cloth. As one would expect, Manymen's output combination is heavily weighted with cloth (the labor-intensive product), and Fewmen's output combination is heavily weighted with cars (the capital-intensive product).

Table 2-2 FACTOR ENDOWMENTS
AND OUTPUT COMBINATIONS

Factors and Products	Manymen	Fewmen
Factor supplies:		
Machines (number)	600	900
Labor (man-years)	6,000	4,500
Machines per man-year	0.1	0.2
Full-employment output combination:		
Cars (number)	4,000	9,000
Cloth (yards)	8,000,000	3,000,000
Cars per thousand yards of cloth	0.5	3.0

17

Clearly, these two countries could gain from trade and would, indeed, be led to trade when brought into contact with each other. Having identical tastes and different output combinations, they would have different price ratios in the absence of trade. Cloth, the labor-intensive good, would be cheap in Manymen, the labor-abundant country, while cars, the capital-intensive good, would be cheap in Fewmen, the capital-abundant country. With the opening of trade and the establishment of common prices, Manymen would specialize in cloth production and would export its specialty in exchange for cars, while Fewmen would specialize in cars and would export its specialty in exchange for cloth. Trade would allow each country to obtain the product it is ill-equipped to manufacture for itself—the one that makes the heaviest demands on its scarce factors of production.

Once again, a free-trade regime is best for the two countries taken together. As in the labor-cost model studied earlier, it works to maximize global output by fostering the most efficient patterns of specialization.

Factor Substitution and Specialization

The numerical example we have been examining can be recast geometrically and can then be made somewhat more general. To do so, let us rearrange the "machines-in-use" identity so as to show how much cloth could be produced if the supply of machinery were the only effective constraint on a country's production:

$$\text{Millions of Yards of Cloth} = \left(\frac{\text{Machines in Use}}{30}\right) - \left(\frac{90}{30}\right) \text{Thousand Cars}$$

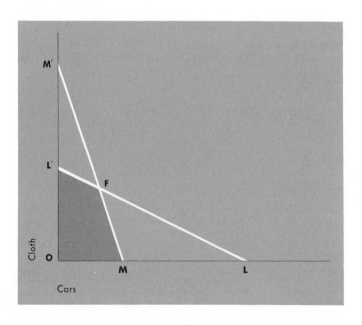

FIG. 2-4 The interaction of technology and factor endowments. A fixed labor supply and fixed labor requirements in car and cloth production impose a labor constraint on production, LL'. A fixed capital supply and fixed capital requirements impose capital constraint, MM'. Taken together these constraints limit production to the region L'FM.

This capital constraint is represented by the line MM' in Fig. 2-4. Next, let us rearrange the "labor-employed" identity to show how much cloth could be produced if the supply of labor were the only effective constraint:

$$\text{Millions of Yards of Cloth} = \left(\frac{\text{Labor Employed}}{600}\right) - \left(\frac{300}{600}\right) \text{Thousand Cars}$$

This labor constraint is represented by LL' in Fig. 2-4.

These two constraints, taken together, define a production-possibilities frontier for a two-product, two-factor country. That frontier is $L'FM$, and the full-employment point occurs at the kink, F. To the left of the kink, production is constrained by the country's limited supply of labor; to the right of the kink, it is constrained by the limited supply of machines. Were such a country unable to engage in trade, its car and cloth consumption would be confined to a combination on or inside $L'FM$. But were it allowed to trade, it could consume a combination of cars and cloth lying outside $L'FM$. If, for instance, world prices permitted the exchange of a single car for a thousand yards of cloth, that country could consume any combination of cars and cloth lying on WW' in Fig. 2-5, and it could escape the limitations imposed by its factor endowment: it could consume Og cars and Oh cloth by exporting gn cars in exchange for mh cloth; it could consume Oj cars and Ok cloth by exporting km cloth in exchange for nj cars.

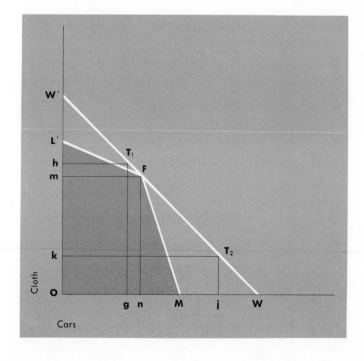

FIG. 2-5 Production and trade with fixed techniques. With a production-possibilities frontier like $L'FM$ and an international price ratio given by the slope of WW', a country could consume at T_1 by exporting gn cars and importing mh cloth, or could consume at T_2 by exporting km cloth and importing nj cars.

Notice, however, that the country portrayed by Figs. 2-4 and 2-5 has one and only one full-employment point, F. Were it to respond to consumer demand or to opportunities for trade by producing more than Om cloth and less than On cars, some of its machines would stand idle and their owners would suffer financial losses. This result derives from an unrealistic assumption regarding technology: that the labor and capital requirements of car and cloth production are entirely rigid. Such a result would not occur at all if manufacturers were able to alter their methods of production. In such circumstances, the owners of idle machines would cut back their rental rates, so as to secure jobs for their machines, and the manufacturers of cars and cloth would respond by choosing more *capital-intensive* methods of production: they would substitute machinery for labor.

When this sort of *factor-substitution* is possible, the factor-endowments model changes in two ways. First, the production-possibilities frontier becomes a smooth curve like $XQPY$ in Fig. 2-6. Second, the domestic price of cars expressed in terms of cloth comes to depend on the output mix, and will equal the slope of $XQPY$ at the point of actual production. If, for example, production were at P, involving Ox_1 cars and Oy_1 cloth, the price of cars in terms of cloth would equal the slope of $XQPY$ at P. If, instead, production were at Q, involving Ox_2 cars and Oy_2 cloth, the price of cars would equal the slope of $XQPY$ at Q.

The curve $XQPY$ is steeper at Q than at P, implying a higher price for cars, and more cars are made at Q. The price of cars must rise to stimulate

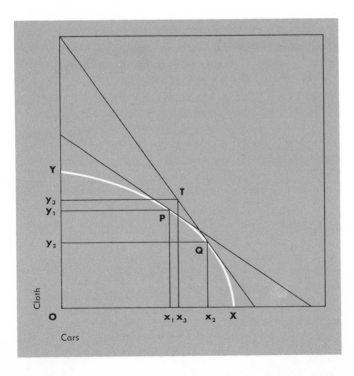

FIG. 2-6 Production and trade with variable techniques. With a production-possibilities frontier like $XQPY$, a country can produce and consume at P (making Ox_1 cars and Oy_1 cloth); the price of cars in terms of cloth will then be equal to the slope of $XQPY$ at P. With trade at a higher price for cars, production will shift to Q (to Ox_2 cars and Oy_2 cloth), and consumption will shift to T (to Ox_3 cars and Oy_3 cloth). The country will export x_2x_3 cars and import y_2y_3 cloth. The precise location of T will depend on demand conditions at home and abroad.

production. This link between prices and the product mix arises from the difference in capital-intensities between the two industries. Cars are more capital-intensive than cloth at all sets of factor prices, so that a switch from cloth to car production will augment the demand for machines relative to the demand for labor. An increase in demand for machinery will bid up rental charges relative to wage rates, and this increase in rental charges will raise the price of cars more than it raises the price of cloth—precisely because car production uses more machinery than cloth production.

Trade and Factor Prices

There is, in fact, a strong connection between prevailing product prices (cars and cloth) and prevailing factor prices (labor and machines), and this connection has an intriguing corollary: *Free trade will tend to equalize factor prices across the participating countries.*

To illustrate this proposition, consider once again our imaginary countries, Manymen and Fewmen. If those two countries have identical tastes and each one is compelled to satisfy its own needs, wages will be low in Manymen relative to rental rates on machinery, and wages will be high in Fewmen relative to rental rates. If the two countries can trade with each other, Manymen can relieve its shortage of machinery by importing the capital-intensive product (cars), and its wages will rise relative to rental rates. Fewmen can likewise relieve its shortage of labor by importing the labor-intensive product (cloth), and its wages will fall relative to rental rates.

This is what free trade will do. As wages would be relatively high in Fewmen before trade began, cloth would be expensive compared to cars. With the opening of trade, Fewmen will therefore export cars and import cloth. To do so, it will increase its car production and cut back its cloth production. These shifts in the pattern of production will, in turn, augment Fewmen's demand for machines and will reduce its demand for labor. Manymen, by contrast, will increase its cloth production and cut back its car production, and these shifts will augment its demand for labor and will reduce its demand for machines. If there are no transport costs between the two countries, free trade will equalize product prices in Fewmen and Manymen. It will thereby equalize the two countries' factor prices.

In actual practice, of course, factor prices are *not* equal around the world—and the differences are far too great to be explained by transport costs and trade barriers. Hence, the simple model we have been developing cannot be perfectly applicable to the real world; it may ignore important economies of scale, and the fact that modern technology is not available to every country. Yet the *tendency* described by the Heckscher-Ohlin model—the *reduction* of factor-price differences through trade—may still be quite important.[6]

[6] Furthermore, available statistics may exaggerate international differences in factor prices. When we compare wage rates around the world, we are comparing rather

Suppose, again, that cars and cloth cannot move between the countries. Wages would be higher in Fewmen than Manymen, and if there were no travel costs, workers would migrate from Manymen to Fewmen. If, further, this migration were to continue for as long as wage rates differed, it would render the two countries very much alike. Fewmen would wind up with as many machines and very much more labor than it had to start with, but the *ratio* of man-years to machines would be exactly equalized in the two countries. This is because the wage-rate difference causing migration would persist for as long as the ratio of man-years to machines were lower in Fewmen than in Manymen. It would only vanish when the ratios were equalized.

This example suggests one more way to look at the gains from trade. It argues that free trade can sometimes substitute for international movements of labor and capital. Factor movements and free trade each serve to reduce differences in factor prices. Factor movements do so by erasing differences in national factor endowments. Free trade does so by offsetting those differences. Trade eliminates the need for a redistribution of productive factors by reallocating economic tasks. It allows every country to make the best use of its own factor endowment.

THE USE
AND ABUSE OF TARIFFS

All the models you have seen illustrate the same basic proposition: *Free trade maximizes world output.* Furthermore, those models show that free trade is beneficial to all of the participating countries. Each country can escape the confines of its own resource endowment to consume a collection of commodities better than the best it can produce.

Why, then, do we still hear so much clamor for protective tariffs and other trade barriers? The answer to this question has two parts. Many fallacious arguments against foreign trade are easily refuted but have a peculiar immunity to logic. Economists can demolish the protectionists' arguments, but speeches about "cheap foreign labor" and the "imperatives of national defense" have enormous popular appeal. Furthermore, several of the arguments for tariffs survive rigorous analysis. Free trade may be best for the world as a whole, but it may not be best from a single country's standpoint: tariffs and other trade barriers may sometimes be employed to redistribute

---

different things. Some countries' wage statistics are heavily weighted with large returns to skill; others' are dominated by the lower wages of unskilled labor. If one were to compare the wage rates of equally skilled workers, of equally fine land, and so on, being sure to match like with like, factor prices might prove to be more nearly equal than they usually appear.

the gains from trade in favor of one country, to redistribute income within a single country, to stimulate domestic employment, or to facilitate economic development.

The Hardy Fallacies

Every now and then, someone tells you that the United States must use tariffs to protect itself from cheap foreign labor. He is armed with lots of figures about low foreign wages, and his numbers are usually accurate. But his inference is totally wrong. In fact, you encountered the answer to his argument when you learned how trading prices are determined. The very first example in this chapter started by assuming that British and American wage rates were exactly equal before the opening of trade. British wages were £5 a day and the exchange rate stood as $3 per pound, so that British and American wages worked out at $15 a day. But when trade was opened, excess demand raised the American wage, and unemployment reduced the British wage. This result was not a caprice of the market; it served a necessary function. If British wages had not fallen, British potato prices would not have declined, and Britain could not have sold potatoes in order to import American coal. The change in wage rates offset Britain's lower productivity and was vital to the process of adjustment that attends the opening of trade. The "cheap foreign labor" argument for tariffs neglects this important link between wages and efficiency. It regards a systematic wage-rate difference as an unfair competitive handicap when, in truth, the difference is required for trade to take place. Wage-rate difference between countries serves to translate comparative advantage into price, and prices guide the flow of trade.

Other protectionists argue for tariffs in the interests of national security—to protect domestic industries capable of turning out guns and planes when war breaks out. This may be the oldest argument in the protectionists' arsenal, and it must be admitted that it did make sense some time ago when, without its own steel mills, no nation could in fact make guns or planes if cut off from its peacetime suppliers abroad. But the national-defense argument for tariffs makes much less sense today. In the thermonuclear age, a nation's ability to protect itself no longer depends upon its capacity to mobilize civilian industries for arms production. A nation cannot count on having time for the process of conversion—and might not have much industry left to convert after a nuclear attack. In today's world, the weaponry on hand at the outbreak of a major war is apt to be decisive and the peacetime protection of defense-related industries is anachronistic.

One must, of course, contemplate the possibility of "limited" wars, like those in Korea and Vietnam. But such wars are not likely to isolate the United States or other major countries from critical materials and finished manufactures. If, indeed, such a conflict were sufficiently widespread to jeopardize normal sources of supply, it could hardly be contained or fought with conventional weapons, but would "escalate" quite rapidly.

23

Note, finally, that the burdens of national defense ought to be apportioned equitably, whereas tariffs levied to protect critical industries tax the peacetime users of specific products by raising the prices of competitive imports. If, then, an industry must be supported in the interests of national security, it should be subsidized directly, out of the government's general tax revenues.

Tariffs and the Distribution of the Gains from Trade

But what of the "respectable" arguments for tariffs—those that appeal to national gain and survive the economist's rigorous scrutiny? One such argument asserts that a single country can extract larger gains from trade by imposing tariffs on goods from abroad. This resembles the familiar proposition that a monopolist can increase his profits by limiting his sales. By restricting imports with a tax, a country *can* sometimes force down the price at which other countries sell it, and thus improve its *terms of trade*. If it carries the process too far, the loss it suffers by foregoing the consumption of imported products will exceed the gain it takes by reducing foreign prices. The monopolist faces an analogous danger: if he cuts back his output too severely, he will lose more on volume than he gains on price. The fact remains, however: a country that enjoys a strategic position in world trade can rearrange the gains from trade in its own favor by a judicious use of import restrictions.

Figure 2-7 illustrates the use of tariffs to this end, showing trade in cotton cloth between Fewmen and Manymen. As in an ordinary supply-and-demand diagram, the price of cloth is measured on the vertical axis and the quantity of cloth is measured on the horizontal axis. Look first at Panel A of Fig. 2-7, which shows Fewmen's own supply curve of cotton cloth, S_d, and the supply curve of exports from Manymen, S_f. When the price of cloth is OP_1, Fewmen's own producers will supply Ob and Manymen's exporters will supply Oa. The sum of these two quantities is OQ_1 in Panel B, a point on the aggregate supply curve of cotton cloth, S_a, obtained by the addition of S_d and S_f. As Fewmen's demand curve, D_d, intersects S_a at R_1, OQ_1 will be consumed at the price OP_1.

Now suppose that Fewmen imposes a 30 per cent tariff, intercepting that fraction of its citizens' expenditure on cotton cloth bought from Manymen's exporters. The price of cloth in Fewmen has now to exceed the price charged by Manymen; the export supply curve, S_f, must be displaced to S_{f+t} so that ih/ha' is 30 per cent of ha', and the aggregate supply curve, S_a, must shift to S_{a+t}, becoming the sum of domestic supply, S_d, and Manymen's export supply with the tariff, S_{f+t}. Supply and demand will be equal at the point R_2, with the quantity consumed at OQ_2, (equal to Ob' plus Oa') and the price of cloth at OP_2 in Fewmen's own market.

This tariff on cotton cloth has several effects. Because the price of cloth has risen in Fewmen, there has been a drop in Fewmen's cloth consumption

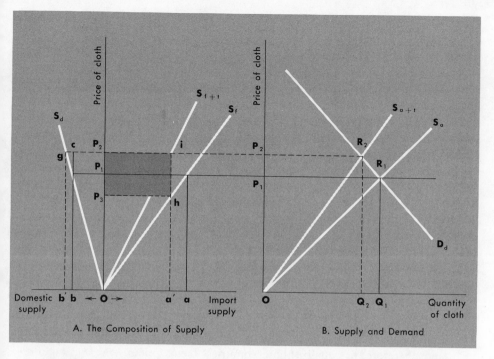

FIG. 2-7 The impact of a tariff on Fewmen's imports and production. A tariff shifts the home-and-import supply curve from S_a to S_{a+t}, raising the domestic price of cotton cloth from OP_1 to OP_2 and lowering the import price from OP_1 to OP_3. Imports are reduced from Oa to Oa' because of the drop in cloth consumption from OQ_1 to OQ_2 and the increase in domestic cloth production from Ob to Ob' (the substitution of domestic production for imports).

by Q_2Q_1 in Panel B. For that same reason, however, there is a new stimulus to local production, and Fewmen's own output has been enlarged by bb' in Panel A. Hence, there is a double squeeze on imports from Manymen—a decrease in consumption and an increase in import-competing production, so that imports from Manymen fall by $a'a$ in Panel A. Finally, Fewmen's government collects P_2P_3 of tariff on each yard of imported cloth, for a total of P_2ihP_3, the shaded area in Panel A.

To complete the analysis of Fewmen's tariff, we would have to allow for the impact of this new tax revenue on Fewmen's fiscal policies. It could spend this revenue or remit it to the public by lowering some other tax; the final equilibrium position depends on its decision. But let us disregard this last refinement and suppose that the point R_2 locates the exact equilibrium position once the tariff is imposed. Notice that the price paid by Fewmen's citizens is higher than it was under free trade (OP_2 is higher than OP_1), but that the price paid to Manymen's exporters is lower than it was under free trade (OP_3 is lower than OP_1). Fewmen is able to obtain its imports more cheaply—at a smaller sacrifice of domestic resources. It has secured better terms of trade.

25

To generalize, a country can capture a larger share of the gains from trade if the foreign supply curve slopes upward and if the foreigner does not retaliate by imposing tariffs of his own. If the foreign supply curve were horizontal, the supply price of imports would not fall (the terms of trade would not improve). If the foreigner were to retaliate, he might recoup his losses, and leave Fewmen worse off than it was with free trade. Fewmen might then impose another round of tariffs and in the end both countries could lose out, for the global gains from trade would shrink as trade was reduced by each successive round of tariffs. Yet governments have sometimes been tempted to use tariffs to improve their terms of trade, and a free-trade situation may not endure unless it is reinforced by international agreements barring the use of tariffs and other trade controls.

Tariffs and the Distribution of Domestic Income

Tariffs can also be employed to alter the domestic distribution of income. Remember that the product-price differences which give rise to trade have their clear counterparts in factor-price differences. Remember, too, that free trade tends to equalize product prices between the participating countries and, therefore, to equalize those countries' factor prices.

Now let us turn the argument on end. Starting with free trade and equal factor prices in Fewmen and Manymen, let Fewmen impose a tariff on imported cloth. This, you have seen, will raise the price of cloth in Fewmen and lower it in Manymen. It will thereby raise the wage rate in Fewmen and will reduce rental rates on machines. The tariff will encourage Fewmen's cloth production and will discourage its car production, for Fewmen's auto exports will contract with the drop in its cloth imports. In consequence, the tariff will increase Fewmen's demand for labor (the input used intensively in cloth production) and will lower its demand for machines (the input used intensively in car production). It will raise Fewmen's wage rates and reduce Fewmen's rental rates, redistributing income in favor of labor.[7]

Equity versus Efficiency

Thus far, you have seen how tariffs can redistribute income between countries and within them. Trade restrictions, however, are a haphazard way to achieve redistribution. Countries with the market power to affect the terms of trade by imposing tariffs—and the pressure groups that influence

---

[7] This argument has its approximate counterpart in Fig. 2-7. The increase in domestic cloth production caused by the tariff (Ob to Ob' in Panel A) will raise the incomes of the factors of production already employed in the cloth industry, even as it adds to production and employment in that industry. Under free trade, the industry was earning a gross income equal to OP_1eb. With a tariff, it will earn OP_2gb'. The increase can be broken down into two parts: $gcbb'$, which goes to the newly employed factors of production (those that produce the extra cloth bb') and cP_2P_1e, which goes to the factors of production *already* employed in making cloth (those that produced the original Ob of cloth).

domestic legislative processes—are not necessarily deserving of aid through redistribution. More importantly, tariffs are an inefficient way to redistribute income. They eat away a part of the pie they are redividing, sacrificing output in the name of equity.

This conclusion follows directly from what you know about free trade. If free trade maximizes global output, any deviation from free trade will reduce world production, leaving less to go around. Figure 2-7 illustrates this point, too. It shows that a tariff replaces low-cost imports with high-cost domestic production. When a tariff is imposed, the last unit of domestic cloth will cost OP_2 dollars to produce (as its price must equal its marginal cost). By contrast, the last unit of imported cloth will cost OP_3 dollars (P_3P_2 dollars less). Hence, the substitution of domestic for foreign cloth fostered by a tariff is wasteful of world resources.

Tariffs and Employment

We have tried to show how tariffs can be used to affect the allocation of resources and the distribution of income. They may also be imposed to affect the *utilization* of resources—the levels of employment and production.

When two countries start to trade, they may not strike an equilibrium right away. One country's prices may be higher than the other's when those prices are compared at the prevailing exchange rate, and that country will be compelled to reduce its wage rates. If it fails to do so, its least efficient industries will shrink, yet its more efficient industries will not grow to take up the slack. The country will trade from a point *inside* its production-possibilities frontier, not from a point *on* that frontier, and free trade may be worse than no trade at all.

If, then, wage rates and other costs are very rigid, a country may gain by restricting its foreign trade. Tariffs will divert demand from foreign to domestic goods, raising domestic output and employment. This result is most likely to occur if the country's unemployed resources are concentrated in its import-competing industries. Tariffs can also combat unemployment caused by a decline in domestic demand during the business cycle, rather than by wage and price disparities revealed at the opening of trade.

Once again, however, tariffs are inefficient policy instruments. They can only stimulate employment by expanding import-competing industries, not the more efficient export industries. Far better, then, to foster wage-rate flexibility or, what may be simpler, to change the exchange rate until a high-cost country's prices are aligned with those of its competitors. Such a country should *devalue* its currency, charging its citizens more for a unit of foreign currency and selling its own currency more cheaply to foreigners. A devaluation raises the domestic price of foreign goods (imports), as foreign currency becomes more expensive. To this extent, it is much like a tariff. But a devaluation also lowers the foreign price of domestic goods (exports), as domestic currency becomes cheaper for foreigners. Unlike a tariff, a devaluation stimulates export industries along with import-competing industries, and does not distort resource allocation.

To put the same point more strongly: tariffs tend to shift one country's unemployment onto its trading partners. One country's import-competing industries (those that benefit from tariff protection) are other countries' export industries (those that make the best use of their resource endowments). Tariffs are a "beggar-my-neighbor" remedy for unemployment.

Tariffs and Economic Transformation

Most of the standard arguments for tariff protection imply a permanent departure from free trade. One group of arguments, however, advocates a *temporary* deviation. From time, to time, it is said, a country must make major changes in its product mix. It must reallocate resources in a large way, not just at the margin, and may find it easier to make the change behind the protection of a tariff wall.

There are two versions of this argument for *transitional* protection: one of them promises economies of scale, the other promises economies of age. The first version reminds us that production costs may rise quite steeply for a while, but will begin to fall when output has attained a level which justifies the use of modern machinery and mass-production methods. It consequently recommends that tariffs be imposed to stimulate domestic production and that those tariffs be retained until the growth of the internal market has allowed domestic firms to imitate the most efficient methods used in other countries. Once they are "over the hump," it is argued, domestic producers will become fully competitive and may even be able to export, so that they will not need permanent protection, and tariffs can be cut.

The second version of the argument urges protection for an "infant industry," and was given its most famous formulation by Alexander Hamilton in his *Report on Manufactures*. A young industry, it argues, may be less efficient than one which has been long established. It may lack seasoned managers, skilled labor, and reliable suppliers of raw materials. Hence, a young industry may warrant protection until it has matured and cut back its unit costs so as to compete with foreign producers. In effect, this version forecasts that temporary tariffs to young industries will actually expand the production-possibilities frontier, and that world output will then be greater because of the transitional departure from free trade.

Both of these versions enjoy widespread respect, for neither has any analytical defect. But enormous problems must be solved in order to apply them correctly. First, one must decide which industries can capture sufficient economies of scale or economies of age to survive after tariffs have been removed. If a country protects all its young industries, it will waste precious resources; almost any industry can grow if given sufficient protection, but some will not endure when their tariffs end. Next, one must determine how large a tariff is required to foster the development of a healthy infant. Too much protection will encourage an excessive expansion, and the protected industries will contract when tariffs are removed. Finally, one must decide if the gains are worth the cost. The use of tariffs, even temporarily, will reduce world output during the transition and may even reduce the real income of the country applying them. These direct and certain losses must be weighed against the distant and uncertain gains offered by protection.

Transitional protection can also pose practical problems. Few industries will readily concede that they have grown up and do not need their tariffs. During their adolescence, moreover, they will have acquired influential spokesmen in government, having become important to the national or regional economy. It will then be difficult to strip them of their tariffs and expose them to the competition they grew up to face. Finally, some governments seem to believe that tariffs can *create* new industries; they restrict imports even when skilled labor, raw materials, and capital are too scarce to allow industrial development.

In brief, the occasions which justify transitional protection may be quite rare, and an indiscriminate application of transitional arguments may do great damage. As with most other tariff arguments, there may be better ways to reach an objective—ways that do not sacrifice income or invite retaliation.

SUMMARY

The structure and benefits of foreign trade derive from an uneven distribution of natural and man-made resources. Each country's endowment of land, minerals, skills, and machinery equips it to perform certain tasks more efficiently than others. Free trade allows a country to do the work it can do best, then to trade the products of its most efficient industries for those that other countries make more economically. Trade is based on comparative advantage, not absolute advantage. Adjustments in wage rates (or exchange rates) compensate for differences in over-all efficiency, allowing each country to adapt its production to its own resource endowment. The price system supplies the incentives to efficient specialization, and when wage rates are flexible, can also make the over-all cost-price adjustments needed to offset differences in absolute efficiency.

From the standpoint of the world as a whole, free trade is best. It serves to maximize global output and is, therefore, a substitute for factor movements. A single country, however, may be able to improve its own position by restricting its imports—by using protective tariffs or other trade controls to swing the terms of trade in its favor. But a tariff that is levied to redistribute income will also reduce it, and is that much more harmful to other countries. There are similar objections to the other arguments for protective tariffs—for tariffs to alter the domestic distribution of income and to stimulate employment, and there are serious practical objections to the use of tariffs as catalysts to economic growth in developing countries.

29

Problems in Trade Policy

CHAPTER THREE

TARIFF THEORY
AND TARIFF HISTORY

At one time or another, every tariff argument has been invoked to justify high import duties, and some of them have been employed by those who advocate free trade. Modern tariff history, then, is also a history of tariff theory, and shows how economic theory can affect policy.

Divergent Tariff Trends: 1815–1860

During the first half of the nineteenth century, the infant-industries argument for tariffs enjoyed a vogue in the United States. The country had just started its industrial development and sought to shelter its young manufacturer from foreign competition. At about that same time, the distributional argument was used in Great Britain with opposite intent: to reduce existing tariffs. Just as the United States was moving toward protection, Great Britain was moving toward free trade.

The United States had taxed its imports from its very birth as a nation. But its early tariffs, though protective in effect, were chiefly designed to raise revenue for the federal government. In those days there was no income tax, and the government relied on excise levies to finance its spending. Tariffs were the most important of those levies. Taxes on imports were very easy to collect; one had merely to police the ports and coastline. It would have been still

31

easier to tax the country's major exports—cotton and tobacco—but the southern states which grew and sold these products had insisted that the Constitution prohibit export duties. They feared that the federal government, dominated by the more populous North, would seek to pay its way by taxing Southern produce.

By 1815, however, there was strong support for a new tariff law fashioned to protect the young manufacturers of New England and the Middle Atlantic states. The Napoleonic Wars had disrupted ordinary channels of trade, and Jefferson's Embargo, designed to prevent the impressment of American seamen by forbidding them to go to sea, had cut this country off from British textiles and hardware. The wars and embargo were equivalent to *prohibitive* tariffs on imported manufactures, giving American industry unrivaled opportunities for growth. But with the coming of peace and resumption of trade, British goods began again to cross the Atlantic, and American manufactures lost ground. Despite the opposition of the South, which naturally preferred to import cheaper foreign products, Congress levied higher duties on woolens and cottons in 1816 and placed higher taxes on imported glass, iron, and cutlery in 1824.

The North-South controversy over tariffs reached a bitter peak after 1828. In that year, the Southerners sought to outmaneuver their antagonists by amending a pending tariff bill. They proposed high duties on raw wool and other crude materials, hoping that the Northern manufacturers who used those materials would reject the entire tariff bill. But the stratagem failed and the bill became law. Its duties were the highest ever imposed prior to the Civil War (see Fig. 3-1), and it was promptly dubbed "The Tariff of Abominations." It inspired South Carolina's "Ordinance of Nullification," which proclaimed a state's right to abrogate federal legislation, asserting that "the tariff law of 1828, and the amendment to the same of 1832, are null and void and no law, nor binding upon this State, its officers and citizens." But this first overt challenge to federal power met firm resistance from President Andrew Jackson, and the furor died down with passage of a compromise tariff in 1833.

In the 1840's the federal budget developed an embarrassing surplus and the Secretary of the Treasury proposed to forego excess tax revenues by reducing tariffs. The average rate of duty on dutiable imports was brought down toward 26 per cent as protective duties were cut sharply in 1846, and again in 1857. But the United States was still out of step with Western Europe, which was moving closer to free trade.

The free-trade movement started in Great Britain as part of a broader assault on the ancient powers of the aristocracy. It sought to end the political hegemony of the rural gentry, who were the chief beneficiaries of the tariffs on imported grain known as the Corn Laws. As in the United States, therefore, tariff policy was entangled in broad constitutional questions, including the issue of parliamentary reform. But the free-trade movement also owed

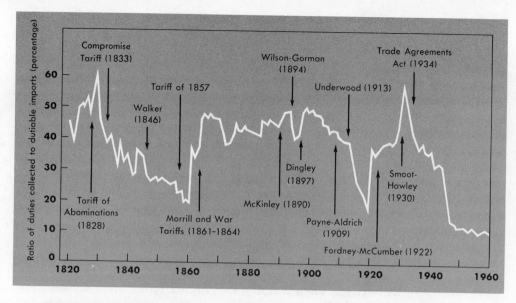

FIG. 3-1 Average U.S. rates of duty on dutiable imports. Legislation raising U.S. duties is usually reflected in an increase in the average on or after passage of the legislation. Legislation cutting U.S. duties is usually reflected in a decline in the average on or after passage. (Source: United States Department of Commerce, Bureau of the Census, *Historical Statistics of the United States* and *Statistical Abstract of the United States*, 1961.)

intellectual debts to Adam Smith, who had made an *allocative* case for free trade fully 50 years before the debates on the Corn Laws:

> What is prudence in the conduct of every private family, can scarce be folly in that of a great kingdom. If a foreign country can supply us with a commodity cheaper than we ourselves can make it, better buy it of them with some part of the produce of our own industry, employed in a way in which we have some advantage. The general industry of the country, being always in proportion to the capital which employs it, will not thereby be diminished . . . but only left to find out the way in which it can be employed with the greatest advantage. It is certainly not employed to the greatest advantage, when it is thus directed toward an object which it can buy cheaper than it can make.

The free-trade movement was further indebted to David Ricardo and other disciples of Adam Smith who made a *distributive* case against the tax on grain. They contended that the Corn Laws were doubly injurious to the wage-earner. First, tariffs raise food prices, reducing the purchasing power of the worker's wage. Second, tariffs increase land rents at the expense of business profits, and low profits mean less saving, less investment, and therefore less demand for labor.

Britain had actually started toward free trade before the Napoleonic Wars. William Pitt had lowered many duties in 1784, and cut back others two years later in the Eden Treaty with France. After the Napoleonic Wars, the Tory government abolished or reduced many duties on industrial raw materials, responding to appeals by the merchants of London, who had a vital stake in free trade. These reductions were supported by Britain's manufacturers, as tariffs on raw materials raised their production costs. They were not opposed by the gentry, who did not produce the materials involved. But during the next decade, attention turned to the tax on grain—a much more explosive issue. In 1842 the Tory government of Sir Robert Peel successfully defeated a Parliamentary motion to repeal the Corn Laws, taking the side of the gentry. But the Irish potato famine of 1845-1846 forced Peel to allow larger grain imports so as to relieve the food shortage. He suspended the Corn Laws in 1845 and split his own party in 1846 by moving for permanent repeal. The Whig governments that followed, led by William Gladstone, completed the task, dismantling most of Britain's other tariffs.

The Triumph and Decline of Free Trade: 1860–1914

In its next step toward free trade, Britain turned from legislation to diplomacy. The Cobden-Chevalier Treaty of 1860 pledged Britain and France to a reciprocal reduction of tariffs, including a reduction in the British tax on French wines. The French then negotiated tariff treaties with other European countries and with the German customs union, or *Zollverein,* organized under Prussian auspices to permit free trade within Germany. The *Zollverein* reduced its external tariffs in exchange for French concessions on German exports.

The commercial treaties of 1860-1870 had two effects. First, they brought about new tariff cuts, enlarging world markets. Second, they *generalized* all of the tariff reductions each country had already made. They included the *most-favored-nation* clause, a standard provision in commercial treaties under which each signatory grants the other every concession given to third countries. Under this clause, France gave the *Zollverein* all of the concessions it had given England in the 1860 treaty. The *Zollverein* was not obliged to make concessions in return, but was committed to grant France the benefits of every tariff cut it had given or would give to any other country.

The free-trade movement, however, was soon to be defeated by a massive and irresistible combination of shifting attitudes and changing circumstances. The 1870's witnessed a sharp change in Europe's colonial policies. Imperialist sentiment had been virtually dormant for half a century, and no major colonies were founded after the Napoleonic Wars, apart from French acquisitions in North Africa. But suddenly the European powers began to scramble for tropical real-estate. The partition of Africa began and was nearly finished in the two decades after 1870. There was renewed rivalry in the Near East and Orient. Bellicose nationalism captured European politics and was soon manifest in measures to protect domestic industry (especially the sectors needed to make armaments) and to obtain control over foreign raw materials.

At about this same time European agriculture experienced a disastrous change of fortune. Railroads and steamships brought wheat from Russia, the United States, and other distant countries into competition with German and

French grain. Even Germany, a major exporter, began to import wheat as farm prices fell. During the decades in which they had exported grain, European farmers and landowners had favored free trade, just like their counterparts in the American South. But when farm prices fell, the farmers changed their minds, and with this change, the balance of political power swung toward protection. In Germany and France alike, a new coalition of nascent industry and injured agriculture reversed the trend in Europe's tariff policies.

The tide turned first in Germany in 1879. Six years earlier, Bismarck had abolished the tariff on iron, and announced that tariffs on iron products would terminate in 1877. But he had over-reached himself, and when the Junkers of the east and farmers of the south united to support the beleaguered manufacturers of the Ruhr and Rhineland, he was forced to backtrack. In 1879, Bismarck brought forward a new tariff affording substantial protection to industry and agriculture.

This new turn toward higher tariffs was defended by invoking the infant-industries argument. That argument, indeed, was given its most elaborate formulation by a German, Friedrich List, who had lived in the United States and was impressed by the rapid growth of its economy behind high tariff walls. He returned to Germany a passionate advocate of infant-industries protection for his native country. List conceded that free trade was best from a cosmopolitan standpoint, but argued that a nation could not afford to heed allocative arguments until it had developed its national industries. Only then, he argued, could a country take its rightful gains from the international division of labor. List's basic point was much like one put forth in Chapter 2: Comparative advantage has a time dimension, and the pattern of trade will reflect the *sequence* of national development. But List went much too far, insisting that countries can only prosper if they export manufactures and import foodstuffs. (Denmark, Australia, and New Zealand give the lie to this assertion; they export farm products yet have higher living standards than many industrial countries.) Unfortunately, List's argument not only won the day, but survives to bedevil economic policies in the less-developed countries of our own era. Many of these countries hanker after massive industries, although they could make better use of their scarce skills and capital. They confuse steel mills and oil refineries with prosperity and national identity.

France followed Germany in 1892, when a coalition of industry and agriculture reversed the low-tariff policies of Napoleon III and enacted the famous Méline Tariff to promote industrial development. The French economy grew rapidly after 1890, but the Méline Tariff cannot take credit for the upsurge. Indeed, it may have handicapped the iron and steel industry, as it levied a high tax on coal, raising the costs of the French iron manufacturers.[1]

---

[1] This point has to be learned anew by every generation, but may perhaps be easier to teach now that the economists have given it a fancy name. The "theory of effective protection" points out that tariffs on an industry's inputs reduce the net stimulus afforded that industry by the tariffs that are levied on its final outputs.

The resurgence of protectionism in the 1890's was followed by a period of tariff warfare involving Germany, Russia, Italy, and other countries. In 1902, Germany actually raised its tariff rates to obtain more leeway for bargaining, and peppered its tariff schedule with trivial distinctions to differentiate the exports of one country from those of another. To distinguish Swiss from Danish cattle, for example, the 1902 tariff had a separate category applying to "brown or dappled cows reared at a level of at least 300 metres above sea level and passing at least one month in every summer at an altitude of at least 800 metres." Hence, a reduction in the German tariff on Danish cattle would not automatically accrue to Swiss cattle under the *most-favored-nation* clause.

American tariffs did not come down as fast or far as European tariffs in the middle third of the nineteenth century. After 1860, moreover, they rose somewhat further. In 1861, Congress passed the Morrill Tariff Act, giving new protection to the iron and steel industry; in 1862 and 1864, it approved a sweeping increase in most other duties. When enacted, these new rates were not designed to grant more protection to American industry but merely to deny the foreigner an unfair advantage over U.S. producers; Congress had imposed heavy excise taxes on many domestic products to finance the Civil War, and the new import taxes were meant to offset them. When the war ended, however, and government spending declined, the domestic excise taxes were allowed to lapse, but the high import duties were not dismantled. They then came to exercise an awesome protective effect. American tariffs reached a post-war peak with the McKinley Tariff of 1890. They were brought down again during Cleveland's second term, when control of Congress passed briefly to the Democrats, but a Republican Congress pushed them to a new peak in 1897.

After 1900, the Republican party seemed to edge away from the extreme protectionism that had been one of its chief tenets. Its 1908 platform declared that "the true principle of protection is best maintained by the imposition of such duties as would equalize the difference between the cost of production at home and abroad, together with a reasonable degree of profit." This formula looked thoroughly reasonable and was reflected in the Tariff Act of 1909, which cut some duties slightly. But what you have already learned about foreign trade should show you that this "scientific" formula will often provide extravagant protection. Differences in costs are the basis for trade, and a tariff designed to offset those differences will therefore prohibit trade, save in tropical products and raw materials that are not produced domestically. If differences in national costs of production are offset by tariffs, transport costs will usually suffice to bar the import of foreign manufactures.

Collapse and Reconstruction: 1914–1939

36   On the eve of the First World War, the United States made a major tariff change. The Wilson administration reduced tariffs drastically in 1913

and added several items to the "free list," including iron, coal, raw wool, lumber, and newsprint. But the end of the World War brought massive new pressures for tariff protection here and abroad.

The war, and subsequent peace settlements, wrecked the international financial system. They disrupted established trade patterns and rearranged capital flows. They burdened the financial system with several layers of debt and large debt-service payments. The Allies had borrowed heavily in the United States to finance their purchases of war materiel. Then, the peace treaties levied reparations debts on the defeated nations. Europe's tariff frontiers were lengthened by some 12,000 miles as the old Habsburg Empire was chopped up into a half-dozen states—Czechoslovakia, Hungary, and the rest—each obliged to make its separate way in the world's market. And some of the victors suffered as much as the vanquished. Britain sold off many of its foreign assets to finance its war efforts, and was thereby deprived of the investment income that had served to offset the pre-war decline in its major export industries.

To make matters worse, many American industries had expanded rapidly during the war, and feared intense competition upon the end of hostilities. This was the case with the chemicals industry, and it was the first to win extra protection after the war. The same thing happened in agriculture, here and in other countries. Encouraged to expand production during the war, farmers confronted ruinous competition afterward and faced adverse terms of trade throughout the 1920's. Rampant inflation compounded the general disorder. In 1923, a German housewife had to carry her money to market in a shopping bag, and could carry her groceries home in a change purse.

One by one, governments levied new tariffs. Some imposed outright import quotas. The new nations of Central Europe were among the first, but were not alone. Germany imposed a new agricultural tariff in 1925. The countries of Latin America applied tariffs and quotas much more freely than they had before the war. And Britain finally lapsed from free trade in 1919 and succumbed to systematic protection in 1931, amidst the general economic crisis.

The United States should have lowered its tariffs after the war, so that the outside world might earn more dollars to service its debts. Instead, Congress voted higher duties during the very first post-war slump. The Fordney-McCumber Tariff of 1922 was designed to aid the farmers, but also helped the chemicals industry and other "war babies."

The trend toward agricultural protection and quantitative trade controls continued in the second half of the decade. It was capped by our own Hawley-Smoot Tariff of 1930, once called the "Holy Smoke Tariff" by an undergraduate with more perception than memory. Congress began hearings on tariff reform in 1929, again intent on helping the farmers. But then the stock market collapsed and the economy began its sickening slide toward the Great Depression. One industry after another clamored for protection to stimulate

37

employment, and when the new tariff bill was laid before Congress, an orgy of logrolling began. Congressmen traded votes with one another, seeking higher tariffs for their own constituents. When it was all over, the United States had the highest tariff in its history, and other countries were compelled to impose additional restrictions on imports from the United States. The Hawley-Smoot Tariff dashed all hopes for global recovery through expanded trade—hopes that had been fostered by the League of Nations' efforts to achieve a tariff truce.

The early 1930's gave birth to a new generation of trade controls. Struggling to prevent the spread of the depression, country after country cracked down on imports, seeking to stimulate domestic production by protecting business against foreign competition. Each in turn frustrated its neighbor's efforts; a fall in one country's imports meant a fall in another country's exports. And after Great Britain had devalued the pound in 1931 and the United States had devalued the dollar in 1934, France and other European countries began to use import controls to defend their currencies.

Foreign trade lagged far behind industrial production in the slow recovery from the Great Depression. It was, indeed, a drag rather than a stimulant to faster expansion. In 1928, world imports had totaled $60 billion; in 1938, they were a mere $25 billion—less than half the pre-depression level.

After 1932, U.S. import duties started to decline. A part of this reduction was caused by an increase in prices during the recovery. Many U.S. tariffs are *specific* duties, fixed in cents per pound, dollars per dozen, and so on. When prices fall, their *ad valorem* (percentage) equivalents rise; when prices rise, those equivalents fall. A 50¢ tariff on a $10 product works out to 5 per cent; if the price falls to $5, the duty works out to 10 per cent; if the price rises to $20, the duty works out to 2.5 per cent.

But the decline in American tariffs was also caused by a major turnabout in policy. Casting about for ways to increase employment, the Roosevelt administration finally turned to world markets, launching a campaign to reduce trade barriers and expand U.S. exports. In 1934, President Roosevelt asked Congress for the power to negotiate bilateral trade agreements that would cut American tariffs by as much as half in return for equivalent reductions by other countries. The President told Congress:

> A resumption of international trade cannot but improve the general situation of other countries, and thus increase their purchasing power. Let us well remember that this in turn spells increased opportunity for American sales. . . . Legislation such as this is an essential step in the program of national economic recovery which the Congress has elaborated during this past year.

Roosevelt promised that tariff reductions would not injure American producers—that he would not open American markets to competitive imports. In effect, he foreswore the allocative gains from trade, looking instead for effects on employment through an expansion of exports. He apparently planned to bargain away our *surplus* protection—the rates that could be cut without attracting imports. Congress gave him the powers he wanted, and the United States negotiated 31 trade agreements with other governments. In each case, moreover, it extended its own concessions to other trading countries under the *most-favored-nation* clause. The Trade Agreements Program was much like the network of treaties that spread out from France following the Cobden-Chevalier Treaty of 1860. Unlike that earlier system, however, it did not bring the nations close to free trade: in 1939, the average U.S. tariff was just below what it had been a decade before, on the eve of the Hawley-Smoot debacle.

The Trade Agreements Program did, however, help to arrest the world-wide increase in tariffs that had been choking world trade. It also held our own tariffs down during and after the Second World War. (After every other major war, by contrast, the U.S. tariff had risen substantially.) This accomplishment was all the more impressive because the inflation of the 1940's greatly reduced the *ad valorem* value of specific duties. By 1945, the average American tariff was as low as it had been in 1919 (see Fig. 3-1).

THE MULTILATERAL APPROACH
TO TRADE POLICY

The American Initiative

The Second World War damaged world trade even more than had the Great Depression. Most of the belligerents imposed strict *exchange controls* to prevent their citizens from spending foreign currencies needed to purchase war materiel and food. They then carried their controls into the post-war period in order to save scarce foreign currencies for their reconstruction programs.

Very early in the war, however, experts began to draw plans for the liberalization of foreign trade and payments in the post-war period. Even before the fighting stopped, the Allied governments established two new financial institutions, the International Monetary Fund (IMF) and the International Bank for Reconstruction and Development (IBRD), to revive and sustain the payments system and to encourage flows of long-term capital. They also planned to promote a fast recovery of world trade by joint action to relax the complex controls that had slowed recovery in the 1930's and strangled trade during the war.

The experts found serious flaws in the pre-war Trade Agreements Program. Many governments had withheld tariff concessions from the United States to save some bargaining power for subsequent negotiations with other countries. The wartime planners consequently urged the use of *multilateral* agreements rather than a new set of country-by-country pacts. Each government might then weigh all it had won—the concessions it had obtained directly in return for its own, and those it had obtained indirectly under the *most-favored-nation* clause. The experts also sought ways to remove the import quotas, payments agreements, and other trade controls that had been used abroad in lieu of tariffs. Quotas frustrate the price system by barring imports, no matter how cheap. Tariffs, by contrast, handicap the foreigner but do not freeze trade patterns or prevent price changes from affecting the allocation of resources. Furthermore, quotas were sometimes used to nullify negotiated tariff cuts: governments imposed import quotas after they had cut their duties. The United States consequently sought a comprehensive agreement on commercial policy, and not just new tariff treaties.

The new U.S. trade policy found its first expression in wartime agreements between the United States and Great Britain—in the Atlantic Charter and Lend-Lease Agreement. It was then embodied in a charter for an International Trade Organization (ITO) to be affiliated with the United Nations. But the ITO never came into being. Its charter was too long and complicated, and was perforated by a host of exceptions and qualifications. It antagonized the foes of international cooperation, who charged that the ITO would meddle with domestic economic policies. It antagonized the advocates of cooperation, who complained that the exceptions and qualifications had swamped the principles, and that no one would be bound to obey the rules.

In 1947, however, the major trading countries were able to agree on interim rules, and began a series of conferences to reduce tariffs and to dismantle other barriers. This interim arrangement has survived, and is known as the General Agreement on Tariffs and Trade (GATT). The GATT is a comparatively simple document; it does not seek to deal with every issue or to anticipate every contingency. Its heart is the *most-favored-nation* clause which provides that every tariff bargain made at GATT meetings shall be extended to all member countries. The GATT commercial code outlaws discriminatory tariffs and prohibits the use of import quotas except by countries experiencing balance-of-payments problems, or by those imposing similar quotas on domestic production—on farm products, for example. It allows the less-developed countries to protect their infant industries, but subjects them to regular GATT review. Finally, it provides machinery to resolve disputes arising from trade policy. During recent years, for example, it has been disentangling problems raised by the creation of the European Economic Community, or Common Market. The formation of the Common Market has threatened the interests of outsiders, including the United States, and GATT members have asked the European countries to adjust their policies so as to minimize damage and dislocation.

Obstacles to Tariff Bargaining

40   In 1945, Congress passed another Trade Agreements Act, authorizing the President to reduce American tariffs through new international bargaining.

The United States then took part in several GATT conferences. In 1950-1951, for example, it made concessions to 22 countries covering a third of its dutiable imports from those countries. To see how these GATT meetings affected U.S. tariff rates, compare the last two columns in Table 3-1; duties declined in every major category, and some rates fell substantially.

Table 3-1   TARIFF REDUCTIONS SINCE 1934, BY COMMODITY CLASS
(Duties collected as a percentage of 1952 dutiable imports)

Commodity Class	1934	1945	1953
All dutiable imports	24.4	17.9	12.2
Chemicals, oils, and paints	25.1	20.0	12.4
Earthenware and glassware	40.6	36.7	24.7
Metals and metal products	23.7	18.9	12.1
Wood and wood products	10.9	7.5	4.7
Sugar and molasses	25.8	13.5	9.4
Tobacco and tobacco products	45.6	34.7	20.3
Agricultural products	16.2	12.5	9.4
Spirits, wines, and other beverages	81.4	41.6	23.1
Cotton products	36.8	30.0	21.8
Flax, hemp, and jute	12.2	9.0	5.2
Wool and wool products	36.7	30.2	22.4
Silk products	58.8	52.7	31.0
Synthetic-fiber textiles	32.8	31.0	17.7
Pulp, paper, and books	20.4	15.2	9.4
Sundries	31.8	26.5	19.1

Source: United States Tariff Commission, "Effect of Trade Agreement Concessions on United States Tariff Levels," 1954.

American imports did not respond to these post-war tariff cuts until other countries had made good the damage done by war and could augment their exports. Recently, however, dutiable imports have been growing faster than duty-free imports, and there has been a considerable rise in manufactured imports, due partly to the tariff reductions negotiated at GATT meetings.

The early post-war cuts were the ones that mattered most. In fact, U.S. tariffs hardly changed between the GATT negotiations of 1950-1951 and those of 1960-1961 with the Common Market. The American negotiators could not offer large reductions in the 1950's, because Congress had hobbled them by amending the Trade Agreements Act.

When President Roosevelt first asked for the authority to reduce U.S. tariffs, he promised that no injury would befall American industry. When President Truman requested additional tariff-cutting powers in 1945, he renewed this pledge. But Truman's assurances did not satisfy Congress, and when the Trade Agreements Act had to be renewed again in 1947, the President was compelled to introduce formal procedures for dealing with injury. He asked the Tariff Commission, a six-man board appointed by the President, to weigh any evidence of injury brought forward by individual industries, and when it had sufficient evidence, to recommend an increase in tariffs or other import restrictions. The President reserved the right to set aside its findings, but had put himself on the defensive. He would henceforth have to justify refusing additional protection.

Protectionist sentiment grew stronger in the early 1950's. With the reconstruction of war-damaged industries abroad, American producers began to meet vigorous competition from Europe and Japan. In addition, labor unions were beginning to worry about low foreign wages. And some Southern congressmen had abandoned their historic opposition to high tariffs; as the South experienced industrial development, they rediscovered the infant-industries argument. In 1951, Congress wrote an *escape clause* into the Trade Agreements Act, formalizing the procedures established by the President and listing the criteria to be used in appraising a complaint of injury:

> In arriving at a determination . . . the Tariff Commission, without excluding other factors, shall take into consideration a downward trend of production, employment, prices, profits, or wages in the domestic industry concerned, or a decline in sales, an increase in imports, either actual or relative to domestic production, a higher or growing inventory, or a decline in the proportion of the domestic market supplied by domestic producers.

Notice that an increase in imports was to be regarded as a *measure* of injury, not just a cause, and that it did not have to be an absolute increase or at the expense of domestic production. A company could petition for higher tariffs if its sales had increased but imports had increased faster.

In 1955 and 1958, Congress broadened the escape clause and made it more difficult for the President to reject the advice of the Tariff Commission. It also wrote a National Security Amendment into the law:

> . . . The President shall . . . give consideration to domestic production needed for projected national defense requirements, . . . existing and anticipated availabilities of the human resources, products, raw materials, and other supplies and services essential to the national defense, and the requirements of growth in such . . . supplies and services including the investment, exploration, and development necessary to assure such growth, . . . and shall take into consideration the impact of foreign competition on the economic welfare of individual domestic industries . . . in determining whether such weakening of our internal economy may impair the national security.

This amendment made very little sense. Economists have always endorsed the protection of defense-related industries. Adam Smith himself supported Britain's *Navigation Acts* because "the defense of Great Britain . . . depends very much upon the number of its sailors and shipping." In our day, however, a nation's security depends on the arsenal of weapons it has built up before hostilities start. This country's power to combat aggression is not enhanced by protecting the domestic producers of watches, lead and zinc, or oil, and sustaining their skills for use in arms production the day after someone has dropped The Bomb. But the sweeping phrases of the National Security Amendment were really designed to serve a more general purpose—to erect one more barrier against import competition. Incidentally, it has been invoked only once—to put quotas on imports of petroleum, including residual fuel oil used in household and industrial furnaces. These quotas were ostensibly designed to stimulate the search for additional domestic petroleum deposits, but also protected the soft-coal industry which has been badly injured by the change-over from coal to fuel-oil.

The escape clause and National Security Amendment gave relief from injury after it had happened—so another clause was added to the Trade Agreements Act to forestall injury. This clause, the *peril-point* provision, directed the President to list all the products on which he planned to make concessions at GATT meetings, so that the Tariff Commission might decide what duties might be needed to prevent injury. The President could then cut a tariff far below its "peril point"—though he would be obliged to give his reasons in a special message to Congress.

These post-war amendments to U.S. trade policy prevented large-scale tariff reductions for a full decade. Furthermore, several of our duties were raised, damaging U.S. relations with friendly countries. Switzerland was injured and offended by an increase in the tariff on watches. Belgium expressed serious doubts about our sincerity in tariff bargaining when, just after making a major agreement with the European Common Market, the United States applied new tariffs to Belgian carpets. The escape clause and National Security Amendment also served to warn our trading partners that past tariff concessions might be snatched away if they were exploited too successfully, while the peril-point provision sometimes caused other countries to withhold concessions because the United States could not reply in kind. In 1960-1961, for example, the Common Market proposed a 20 per cent reduction in its common external tariff if the United States would make a similar reduction. When it became clear that the American negotiators could not make so broad a cut, the Europeans pared down their offer.

The European Initiative

Each time the White House asked for a renewal of the Trade Agreements Act, a parade of industry spokesmen appeared before congressional committees to demand more protection and to denounce low tariffs as the source of all their woes. Each time, the administration purchased a renewal of its bargaining powers by agreeing to amendments that restricted its freedom of action and provided easier ways to redress injury.

Yet the advocates of liberal tariff policies were not wholly dissatisfied with this ritual. They argued that tariffs were not too important—that quotas and limitations on the convertibility of foreign currencies were doing much more damage to world trade. They also pointed out that few foreign countries

43

could offer much in tariff bargaining, for their markets were too small. These were valid views of the situation in the early 1950's. But as the United States marked time in trade policy, events in Europe were undermining the premises of U.S. policy. European governments were making dramatic decisions that would change the balance of advantage in tariff bargaining. Today, most experts would agree, American industry has far more to gain than lose from new negotiations.

At the close of the Second World War, the United States began an unprecedented financial effort to reconstruct Western Europe. This was the Marshall Plan. At the same time, it urged the Europeans to combine their resources and realize an age-old dream: a United States of Europe. Washington was much concerned to strengthen Europe against Soviet aggression, and, as urgently, to enlist Germany in a democratic federation so that it might never destroy the peace again.

At first, the Europeans started to integrate one industry at a time—the sector-by-sector approach to unification. They established a European Coal and Steel Community, making for free trade in coal and steel and creating a supranational High Authority with the power to regulate pricing policies and commercial practices. Then they changed their tactics and began to work for a full *customs union* of six continental countries—France, Germany, Italy, the Nethelands, Belgium, and Luxembourg. In 1957 these countries signed the Treaty of Rome, establishing the European Economic Community (EEC), or Common Market. They agreed to eliminate all barriers to trade among themselves and to surround themselves with a common external tariff—a set of duties constructed by averaging their separate national tariffs. They also agreed to "harmonize" domestic policies, including agricultural policies; to lift their restrictions on movements of men and money inside Europe; and to plan for political unification. A year later, the Europeans took another major step. They made their currencies convertible, removing any cause for continued discrimination against American goods. Once all their currencies could be used to buy dollars, no country had reason to require that its citizens buy European goods to conserve dollar earnings. In consequence, most countries lifted their import quotas.

For many Europeans, and for Washington as well, eventual political unification is the chief rationale for the EEC. But the member countries also hope to reap large economic gains. They expect to sharpen business competition, thereby to foster a more efficient use of resources and a better allocation of economic tasks. They expect to capture the economies of scale often associated with larger markets and, in consequence, to strengthen European firms *vis-à-vis* the "giant-sized" American companies. The European Common Market has a combined population of about 185,000,000 and a gross regional product approaching $300 billion; it is nearly as populous as the United States, and is almost half as wealthy.

The transition to internal free trade and policy harmonization has been neither smooth nor painless. It has in fact been punctuated by several crises, the first of which occurred in 1963 when France exercised its veto power to reject a British application for membership. A second arose from deep-seated differences regarding agricultural prices, and that has not yet been fully resolved. The Treaty of Rome requires that the EEC institute a common agricultural policy. To that end, its members must agree on the levels at which prices shall be supported and on a distribution of the costs to be incurred in maintaining price supports. Agreement has been difficult, partly because Germany has sought to protect its farmers from a rapid growth of grain exports from France. Moreover, lurking behind such particular issues is a more serious general obstacle to policy harmonization: the French government of General DeGaulle has been deeply suspicious of all supranational arrangements, for these involve a sacrifice of national autonomy. It has sought to curb the powers of the EEC Commission, the civil service of the Community. So far, however, all of these crises, and others as well, have been resolved or postponed, and the EEC has come very close to its initial objective: the creation of a common market for merchandise trade.

The near-formation of this common market and the restoration of convertibility have left tariffs as the major barriers to trade, and tariff policy has begun to matter once again. Moreover, the EEC is a constellation of countries and markets large enough to bargain with the United States. And all of these developments have helped to foster rapid economic growth in Western Europe, creating unprecedented opportunities for American industry. There has been a heavy flow of private American capital to the EEC countries, as hundreds of companies have built factories there. Many American industries now manufacture more abroad than they export from their plants in the United States, and overseas production continues to grow very rapidly. The exports listed in Table 3-2 are 60 per cent larger than they were in 1957, but the overseas production has doubled.

Table 3-2 U.S. EXPORTS OF SELECTED MANUFACTURES AND PRODUCTION BY U.S. COMPANIES ABROAD, 1964 (Millions of dollars)

Product Class	U.S. Exports	Production Abroad
Paper and allied products	596	1,510
Chemicals	2,345	5,945
Rubber products	362	1,605
Non-electrical machinery	4,704	4,650
Electrical machinery	1,284	3,340
Transportation equipment	1,733 *	9,480
All items	11,024	26,530
Of which Europe	3,177	12,210

* Excluding civilian aircraft.

Source: United States Department of Commerce, Survey of Current Business, November, 1965.

The European Economic Community, then, presents a new challenge to American trade policy. Although its common tariff may not be more restrictive than the separate national tariffs from which it was built, that new tariff can do damage to important trade patterns. Before the creation of the EEC, American, German, and Italian goods paid the same duties when they entered France. Soon, German and Italian products will not pay any duties, while American products will still be taxed, along with those of other outsiders, who depend heavily on European markets. To complicate matters, the EEC has granted "associate" status to several developing countries, most of them in Africa, and admits their exports on better terms than those enjoyed by other developing countries, notably those of Latin America.

The Trade Expansion Act of 1962

Responding to these developments, the Kennedy administration sought new tariff legislation, and in the Trade Expansion Act of 1962, Congress authorized the president to cut U.S. tariffs once again. In fact, it gave him much more power than it had conferred by any single tariff law since the original Trade Agreements Act of 1934. Heretofore the United States had bargained on a rate-by-rate, product-by-product basis; henceforth, it could make more sweeping agreements: it could cut *all* its tariffs in half, in return for similar "across-the-board" reductions by other countries. Furthermore, the Trade Expansion Act modified the basic "no injury" rule that had hobbled U.S. negotiators and impaired the logic of our tariff policy. A country exports so that it can import, yet the old Trade Agreements Acts were chiefly concerned to stimulate exports. They looked on additional imports as the price we had to pay to widen our export markets—and one we would not pay if increased imports damaged domestic industry. The 1962 law makes much more sense. First, it redefines injury from imports, instructing the Tariff Commission to require evidence that men and machines have actually been idled by foreign competition—not merely that prices have fallen or that imports have grown faster than domestic production. Second, it provides new ways to deal with injury. Instead of imposing additional tariffs, the President may authorize direct assistance: extended unemployment compensation and retraining for workers; tax benefits and loans for employers, to help them diversify or modernize their plants. Thus, it seeks to capture the allocative gains from trade by fostering changes in resource use, rather than renouncing those important gains by restricting foreign trade and subsidizing inefficient industries.

Soon after the passage of the Trade Expansion Act, a new round of bargaining got underway. It was interrupted several times by the crises besetting the Common Market, but gained momentum in 1966. At the time this book came off the presses, the outcome was not certain. The Trade Expansion Act was due to expire in mid-1967. But there was cause for optimism, because all sides agreed that the collapse of the so-called "Kennedy round" would mean a major setback for the world economy, while freer trade between Europe and the United States would improve the allocation of resources within the industrial world, and would provide the less-developed countries with a new stimulus to economic growth. Tariffs are high enough to restrict world trade, and there are major differences between U.S. tariff rates and those of the EEC, so that the two can bargain to mutual benefit. For instance, the Common Market's tariffs on chemicals, machinery, and vehicles are higher than the corresponding U.S. rates (see Table 3-3), but U.S. duties on textiles and apparel, ceramics and glassware, optical equipment, and watches are higher than those of the EEC.

Table 3-3   U.S. AND COMMON MARKET TARIFFS
ON INDUSTRIAL PRODUCTS
(Percentage equivalents weighted by 1960 imports;
rates in force prior to the 1961 GATT negotiations)

Commodity Class	United States	Common Market
Mineral products	3.0	2.4
Chemicals and allied products	6.9	13.0
Plastics and plastic products	2.7	10.0
Leather and leather products	6.5	2.9
Wood and wood products	6.0	6.1
Pulp, paper, and paper products	0.8	7.9
Textile fibers, textiles, and textile products	19.0	7.5
Stone, ceramic, and glass products	25.8	15.0
Base metals and metal products	7.4	5.9
Machinery and mechanical appliances	10.9	13.8
Vehicles, aircraft, and other transport equipment	10.9	17.5
Optical, photographic and scientific instruments, watches and clocks	25.3	15.9

Source: Committee for Economic Development, A New Trade Policy for the United States, 1962.

Tariff reduction may do damage to some of our industries, but continued protection may not help them much over the long run. Many of the industries most apt to be affected by tariff reductions have been limping along for many years, even with high duties. A recent study of employment in protected industries shows that:

... the heavily protected, import-competing industries are not only predominantly declining, but they are declining more than the less-protected, import-competing industries.[2]

[2] Beatrice N. Vaccara, Employment and Output in Protected Manufacturing Industries (Washington, D.C.: The Brookings Institution, 1960), p. 68.

Another study indicates that the problem of adjustment to increased imports will not be very large.[3] A $1 billion increase in dutiable imports spread across all industries and displacing an equivalent amount of domestic production would decrease employment in many industries:

Gross *decrease* in the import-competing industries	63,000 man-years
Gross *decrease* in other industries	52,000 man-years
Gross *decrease* in all industries	115,000 man-years

But these calculations do not allow for the increase in exports that would follow the reduction of other countries' tariffs, nor for the increase that would occur merely because foreigners were earning more and were willing to spend more on our exports. Notice, further, that a large part of the decrease in employment would be very widely diffused, not wholly concentrated on the import-competing industries. This is because every firm buys materials and services from others.

Admittedly, much of the job loss due to larger imports would focus on a few firms and communities, and many of these are already in deep trouble on account of changes in tastes and technology. In 14 out of 72 industries, a $50 million increase in imports would suffice to double or more than double the gross separation rate (quits and layoffs). Furthermore, trade adjustment programs will not work unless the American economy is growing steadily. Companies will not diversify production if they lack new markets; workers will not benefit from retraining if there are no new jobs. European experience has itself demonstrated that an adjustment to import competition is easiest when aggregate demand is growing rapidly, so that opportunities abound for those who lose their jobs. If indeed there is any reason to insist that the American economy grow fast, it is that rapid growth will permit adjustments to all sorts of disturbances: changes in tastes and technology, and increased import competition. The pull of buoyant demand is much more effective in reshuffling resources than is the sting of shrinking markets and high unemployment.

SUMMARY

The tariff histories of Western Europe and the United States describe very similar cycles. Both histories reflect the influence of economic theory, industrial development, and international politics.

In Europe, tariffs started downward after the Napoleonic Wars, reaching their nadir after 1860. Britain led the way with unilateral reductions; the

[3] The data that follow are taken from Walter S. Salant and Beatrice N. Vaccara, *Import Liberalization and Employment* (Washington, D.C.: The Brookings Institution, 1961), p. 215. They relate to a $1 billion increase of imports at 1953 prices and to the median data for 72 import-competing industries.

continental countries followed suit, using tariff treaties. Tariffs moved up again after 1880, with the re-emergence of aggressive nationalism and shifts in the balance of political power caused partly by shifts in agricultural trade. Trade restrictions became even more severe in the 1920's, and the global depression of the 1930's caused many countries to impose import quotas. These controls remained in force through the Second World War, but were gradually dismantled in the 1950's. Then, Europe began to cut its tariff rates as well, but chiefly in respect to European trade, not on imports from outside. The European Economic Community, or Common Market, is the end-product of this trend. It will eliminate all trade barriers within Western Europe and facilitate the free flow of labor and capital.

In the United States, tariffs moved upward after the Napoleonic Wars, and came down briefly during the 1840's and 1850's, coincident with the repeal of the British Corn Laws. But they moved up again during the Civil War, and did not decline until the eve of the First World War. Afterward, moreover, U.S. tariffs rose again, hitting their all-time high with the Hawley-Smoot Tariff of 1930. Thereafter, the United States negotiated tariff treaties with a large number of countries, and in the 1940's and 1950's participated in new tariff bargaining under the auspices of the General Agreement on Tariffs and Trade. The U.S. program lost momentum in the 1950's as Congress added restrictive amendments to the Trade Agreements Act: the escape clause, the peril-point provision, and the National Security Amendment. In 1962, however, Congress passed new trade legislation, responding to the challenge of the EEC. The President is now empowered to reduce most U.S. tariffs and to assist injured industries directly.

The Balance of Payments

and Foreign-Exchange Market

CHAPTER FOUR

BALANCE-OF-PAYMENTS
ACCOUNTING

Thus far, we have studied the effects of foreign trade on the allocation of resources and distribution of income—always assuming that payments from one country to another are balanced by payments from the second to the first. This vital equality can be secured by wage-rate or exchange-rate changes. In Chapter 2, you will recall, American wage rates and prices were at first so low that consumers in America and Britain both preferred to buy American coal but were indifferent as between American or British potatoes. Trade did not balance. Then the foreign demand for American coal raised America's wage rate until its potatoes became more expensive than British potatoes, and balanced trade ensued. As a matter of actual fact, however, wage rates and prices may not respond smoothly to correct imbalances in international payments. Wages and other costs may be very sticky and may even move independently of demand conditions, *causing* a lopsided flow of payments. Furthermore, some international cash flows will not act on wages and prices so as to restore equilibrium; a demand for foreign securities, for example, will not change wage rates or other costs directly.

Under these circumstances, governments seeking to maintain fixed exchange rates may encounter difficult monetary problems in their relations with the outside world. Economists sometimes de-

51

scribe these problems as "transitional" or "short-run" phenomena that should not divert our attention from the "real" flows of goods, services, and capital. But the "short run" may drag on for a long time, and imperfections in the process of wage, price, and exchange-rate adjustment may often alter "real" flows. If wage rates and exchange rates are rigid, a country may not be able to balance its external transactions at a satisfactory level of domestic employment or may have to forego economic growth. In the late 1950's for example, the condition of the U.S. *balance of payments,* or sum total of American transactions with foreigners, discouraged the government from adopting financial policies to stimulate domestic growth.

As a preface to our study of these monetary issues, we will examine a group of transactions put together in a hypothetical *balance-of-payments* table for the United States. Then we will consider the several ways of balancing the cash flows that arise from these transactions.

A balance-of-payments table is designed to summarize a nation's transactions with the outside world. It is usually divided into three sections:

1. *The current account,* which shows flows of goods and services.
2. *The capital account,* which shows lending and investment.
3. *The cash account,* which shows how cash balances and short-term claims have changed in response to current and capital transactions.

This three-way division is especially convenient for economic analysis. To see how a country's external transactions affect its income and employment, an economist will look at the current account. This account will show total foreign spending on current domestic output, for it will list all exports of domestic goods and services. It will also tabulate a country's total spending on foreign goods and services and, therefore, its contribution to income and employment elsewhere in the world. Notice, incidentally, that most of our work in Chapter 2 dealt with the current account and assumed that current-account outlays (imports) were equal to current-account earnings (exports).

The capital and cash accounts show how foreign trade and payments affect wealth and debt. If American citizens acquire foreign stocks and bonds —claims on foreigners—they will earn income in the future, and when they sell their claims, can import goods and services. If, instead, American citizens borrow from a foreign bank or sell securities to foreigners, they will have to make interest payments in the future, and when their debts come due, must export more to foreigners.

Some foreign debts and claims are easily classified. The purchase of a permanent interest in a foreign company is a long-term capital transaction. The acquisition of a foreign bank balance is a cash transaction. But how should a foreign purchase of a U.S. Treasury bill be classified? It is an earning asset for the foreigner, just like a bond or stock, but is a close substitute for cash because it matures very quickly. Many foreign banks and governments invest their dollar holdings in short-term securities like Treasury bills, rather than holding idle bank deposits. In practice, the dividing line between capital and cash is drawn so that claims and debts maturing in a year or less go into the cash account, and those that mature in more than a year (or have no fixed maturity) go into the capital account. Like any arbitrary rule, this one sometimes leads to strange results. But we need some sort of rule to assure consistency and permit comparisons through time.

Every international transaction will appear in two of the three accounts —or more than once in one account. This is because every transaction involves a transfer of goods, services, or securities against cash or a debt-instrument (an IOU or bank loan). Each one will be entered as a *debit* (with a minus sign) insofar as it enlarges the supply of goods and services available for domestic use, adds to U.S. claims on foreigners, or reduces U.S. debts. Each one will be entered as a *credit* (with a plus sign) insofar as it reduces the supply of goods and services, reduces U.S. claims on foreigners, or increases U.S. debts. To illustrate, consider five transactions:

1. *An American purchase of $280,000 worth of tin from Malaya, paid for with pounds sterling bought with dollars from a New York bank.*

The purchase of tin will appear on current account because it creates income abroad. It will appear as a *debit* there because it enlarges the supply of goods available to Americans. It is listed next to *merchandise imports* in Table 4-1. The transfer of pounds sterling to pay for the tin will appear on cash account as a change in *U.S. holdings of foreign currencies*. It will appear as a *credit* there because it reduces American claims on the outside world (U.S. holdings of pounds sterling). The American importer of tin will go to a New York bank, write a check for $280,000 (plus a small commission), and receive a *draft* for £100,000 drawn on that bank's balance at a London bank. The ratio $280:£100 or $2.80:£1 is the exchange rate between the dollar and the pound. Next, the American importer will transfer the sterling draft to the Malayan tin producer, who will sell it to his bank in Singapore, obtaining the Malayan equivalent of £100,000. To complete the transaction, the bank in Singapore will send the draft to London, where the bank on which it was drawn will deduct £100,000 from the sterling balance of the New York bank that issued the draft.

2. *An American sale of $300,000 worth of antibiotics to Venezuela, paid for with dollars bought from a bank in Caracas.*

The American sale of antibiotics will also appear on current account, because it creates income in the United States. But it will be a *credit* item because it decreases the supply of goods available to Americans. It is listed next to *merchandise exports* in Table 4-1. The transfer of dollars to pay for the drugs will show up in the cash account as a change in *foreign holdings of dollars,* and will be a *debit* there because it decreases American liabilities to the outside world (Venezuelan holdings of dollars). In this case, the Venezuelan importer will buy a $300,000 draft from a bank in Caracas, paying with Venezuelan currency. He will send the dollar draft to the U.S. exporter,

53

Table 4-1 **A HYPOTHETICAL BALANCE-OF-PAYMENTS TABLE FOR THE UNITED STATES** (Thousands of dollars)

Item		Amount
A. Current Account		
Merchandise exports		+500
Antibiotics	300	
Machine tools	200	
Merchandise imports		−280
Tin	280	
Services		+ 50
Ship rental	50	
Balance on current account		**+270**
B. Capital Account		
Direct investment		−400
Factory in Italy	400	
Government lending		−200
Indian loan	200	
Balance on capital account		**−600**
Balance on current and capital accounts		**−330**
C. Cash Account		
Increase (+) in foreign holdings of dollars		+100
Antibiotics	−300	
Factory in Italy	400	
Indian loan	200	
Machine tools	−200	
Increase (−) in U.S. holdings of foreign currencies		+230
Tin	280	
Ship rental	− 50	
Balance on cash account		**+330**

who will deposit it in his own bank. The draft will then be sent to the New York bank at which the Venezuelan bank keeps its dollar balance, and $300,000 will be deducted from the Venezuelan's dollar account.

3. *The leasing of an American ship for $50,000 to carry frozen beef from Argentina to Liverpool.*

This transaction is similar to an export sale; the U.S. ship-owner contracts to provide a service using American resources. Hence, the rental fee will appear as a *credit* on current account. If, next, the Argentine meatpacker leasing the ship pays $50,000 worth of Argentine currency (pesos) and the U.S. ship-owner sells them to his bank, there will be an increase in American holdings of Argentine currency, and this will appear as a *debit* (an increase of American claims on foreigners) in the cash account of Table 4-1.

4. *The building of a $400,000 factory in Italy by an American company, to assemble tractors for sale in the Common Market.*

This transaction also appears in the U.S. balance of payments, although no goods or services cross our own frontier. It represents the acquisition of an earning asset, and will appear as a *debit* on capital account. It is called *direct investment* because it is an outright extension of American enterprise rather than a purchase of securities issued by a foreign firm. The building costs will be reflected in the cash account as a *credit* entry, appearing as an increase in Italian holdings of dollars when the necessary lire are bought with dollars from an Italian bank.

5. *A $200,000 loan from the U.S. Export-Import Bank to the Indian government for the purchase of American-made machine tools.*

Since the Export-Import Bank is an agency of the U.S. government, the $200,000 loan will appear as a government transaction on capital account. It will be a *debit* because it generates a claim on India. It will also give rise to a *credit* on cash account—an increase in Indian holdings of dollars. When, however, the Indian government draws down its dollar balance to buy machinery, a *credit* entry will appear on current account; an export of machine tools will increase American income but reduce the supply of goods available to Americans. A corresponding *debit* entry will appear on cash account.

Now total up the entries in each section of Table 4-1—the current, capital, and cash accounts. Notice that the balance on current account *plus* the balance on capital account must offset the balance on cash account. The excess of American spending abroad, including purchases of long-term earning assets, must match the net change in the American cash position. The United States is $330,000 richer in goods and earning assets, but poorer in cash by a like amount; it owes $100,000 more to foreign banks and holds $230,000 less of foreign currencies. We shall call this reduction in the U.S. cash position the *gross payments deficit*.[1] It measures the gap between gross payments *from* the United States and gross payments *to* the United States, and is the first of two concepts we will employ to measure imbalances in external payments.

In Table 4-1, the United States has a gross deficit even though it also has a current-account surplus. By implication, a country may have a deficit although it is quite capable of earning its way in world markets. Such a country is merely using cash or credit to acquire extra earning assets. This is precisely what the United States has done during recent years, and it is not necessarily a "bad thing." If a country starts out with a strong cash position, it may do well to run a deficit in order to acquire more earning assets. A deficit becomes dangerous only when it cuts so deeply into cash holdings that a country can no longer cope with unplanned deficits arising from cyclical and other disturbances—or when the deficit continues despite every effort to staunch it, so that citizens and foreigners alike begin to doubt the government's ability to control the situation.

A balance-of-payments table is chiefly designed to measure deficits and surpluses with the outside world, but tells us much more.[2] First, the current

---

[1] It is sometimes called the "basic" deficit, but we prefer the term used in the text.

[2] In actual practice, however, the accounts are not drawn up like Table 4-1, transaction by transaction. Instead, the statisticians gather the available data on each

account shows how foreign trade affects total income at home and abroad. In our example, Americans have earned $550,000 by selling goods and services to other countries; foreigners have earned $280,000. Second, the cash account shows what has happened to the public's cash holdings at home and abroad. Foreign banks have acquired an additional $100,000 of dollar balances; these funds came from American firms and households. American banks have lost $230,000 worth of foreign currency; these funds were paid to foreigners. Thus, dollar bank deposits held by Americans have fallen by $100,000, while the foreign-currency bank deposits of foreigners have increased by the equivalent of $230,000. Finally, the cash account shows what has happened to the working balances of foreign currencies held by banks. American banks have run down their balances by the equivalent of $230,000; foreign banks have increased theirs by $100,000.

ALTERNATIVE MONETARY SYSTEMS

The banks' working balances of foreign exchange play a strategic role in the international payments system. Each transaction in Table 4-1 drew upon or added to those balances, as the banks stood by to furnish foreign currencies and U.S. dollars when traders and investors needed them. But the banks cannot let their holdings fall very low because they must have foreign currencies on hand to make future sales. Nor can they allow their balances to rise very high because they would tie up loanable funds in their foreign-exchange business and, more importantly, could suffer losses if exchange rates changed. The banks must keep close control over their inventories. Thus, in Table 4-1, foreign banks might seek to sell all or part of the $100,000 increase in their dollar balances, and U.S. banks might seek to purchase foreign currencies in order to make good all or part of the $230,000 decrease.

Suppose, then, that foreign banks seek to sell $50,000 and that U.S. banks seek to buy $130,000 worth of foreign currencies. The foreign banks will offer $50,000 in the New York foreign-exchange market, in exchange for an assortment of pounds, francs, marks, and other currencies. The American banks will enter the same market offering $130,000 in exchange for a similar assortment. This foreign-exchange market is nothing more than a

type of flow (goods, services, direct investment, and long-term securities transactions), then try to reconcile the balance on current and capital account with the separate banking data on cash holdings. They cannot do this perfectly, as many items escape the statisticians' net. Each country's balance-of-payments table, therefore, has a term that Table 4-1 lacked—an allowance for "errors and omissions" to fill the gap between the recorded surplus or deficit and the net change in the cash position. We will look at an actual balance-of-payments table in Chapter 5 and will find some other differences between Table 4-1 and the real thing.

network of telephone connections among major banks and brokers. But it is much like any other market, where variations in supply and demand lead to price changes. We will, indeed, analyze the foreign-exchange market using supply-and-demand curves.

With foreign and American commercial banks trying to buy $180,000 worth of foreign currencies ($50,000 *plus* $130,000), there will be an *excess demand* for foreign currency (an *excess supply* of dollars) in the foreign-exchange market. Such a situation will touch off a chain of events that will eventually react on the current and the capital accounts in the balance of payments. They will decrease the American demand for foreign currencies and increase the foreign demand for U.S. dollars. They will thereby reduce the gross payments deficit and restore equilibrium in the foreign-exchange market by forestalling further changes in the banks' working balances. But the nature and the sequence of these happenings will depend on the organization of the international monetary system—on the extent to which exchange rates are free to fluctuate and on the way each country's money supply is connected to its gold and foreign-exchange holdings. To illustrate, we shall describe three monetary systems and show how they would operate if there were an excess demand for foreign currency.

1. A system of *flexible exchange rates,* under which the prices of foreign currencies are left to fluctuate when there are changes in supply and demand. Here, exchange-rate changes will operate directly to eliminate any excess demand for foreign currencies. The prices of foreign currencies will rise, making foreign goods more expensive for Americans and making American goods cheaper for foreigners. Americans will buy fewer foreign goods, and foreigners will buy more American goods.

2. A *pure gold standard,* under which the prices of foreign currencies cannot change because every currency has a fixed gold value. If one currency is worth 20 grains of gold and another is worth 10, the first can always be exchanged for 2 units of the second. With an excess demand for foreign currencies, gold will flow out of the United States, reducing its money supply and, therefore, its price level. Entering other countries, it will augment their money supplies and will raise their prices. These price-level changes will work just like exchange-rate changes, making foreign goods more expensive for Americans and making U.S. goods cheaper for foreigners. A gold flow will also alter interest rates and attract short-term capital to the United States.

3. A system of *managed exchange rates,* under which exchange rates are stabilized by official intervention in the foreign-exchange market. Here, too, supplies of money may change, altering prices and the balance of payments. But there may be no strict link between the domestic monetary situation and the foreign-exchange market. Hence, price levels will not necessarily change to combat an excess demand for foreign currencies, and governments may then be compelled to alter exchange rates by changing their foreign-exchange policies.

57

If exchange rates were free to fluctuate, an excess demand for foreign currencies would cause the dollar to *depreciate*. It would depress the price of the dollar in terms of foreign currencies or, what is the same thing, would raise the dollar prices of foreign currencies. This change in exchange rates, in turn, could alter the flow of trade. If the French franc were selling for $0.25 to start, a French car costing 6,000 francs would sell for $1,500. An excess demand for foreign currencies that raised the dollar price of the French franc to $0.40 would raise the dollar price of that French car to $2,400. Americans would buy fewer French cars. Similarly, an American machine costing $10,000 would sell at first for 40,000 francs, but for only 25,000 francs after the depreciation of the dollar. French industry would buy more American machines. These changes in U.S. imports and exports would alter the supply of dollars and the demand for dollars on the foreign-exchange market.

Consider the demand for dollars, analyzed in Fig. 4-1. The vertical axis in Panel A shows the price of an American machine in French francs. The vertical axis in Panel B shows the price of that machine in U.S. dollars. If, for instance, the dollar price of a machine is $10,000 and a dollar will buy 4 French francs, the French franc price of the machine will be 40,000 francs, as shown in Panel A. The horizontal axes of both panels list export volume (the number of machines), and this must be the same in both parts of the diagram. Finally, Panel A shows the French demand for U.S. machines, the curve D_1, which gives an equilibrium at Q_1. The United States will export OA machines, receiving $40,000 \times OA$ francs.

Now let the dollar depreciate in the foreign-exchange market. The dollar price of an American machine need not change at all (U_1 need not shift). But the franc price of that machine has to fall apace with the depreciation. If, then, the depreciation raises the price of the franc all the way to $0.40, the franc price of a single American machine will drop to 25,000 and the supply curve facing French buyers will be S_2 instead of S_1. Equilibrium will be displaced to Q_2, and French imports of American machines will rise to OB.

The number of French francs spent on imports of machines may either rise or fall with the depreciation of the U.S. dollar. (It will fall if rectangle I is larger than rectangle II, and will rise if rectangle I is smaller than rectangle II.) But this ambiguity need not concern us, for we want to measure the change in the demand for dollars, not in the supply of francs. Look, then, at Panel B, and notice that the dollar price of a machine has not changed at all, so that the French demand for dollars is bound to rise when the dollar depreciates. The increase in the French demand for U.S. machines appears as a rightward shift in the demand curve (from E_1 to E_2), and the French demand for dollars grows by $10,000 \times AB,$ equal to the area of rectangle III.

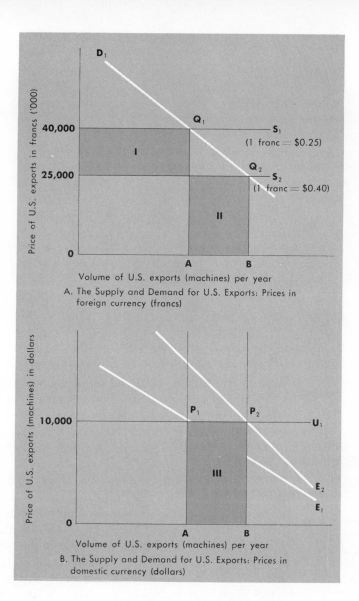

FIG. 4-1 Currency depreciation and the demand for exports. A depreciation of the dollar lowers the franc price of U.S. machines from S_1 to S_2. It will increase total franc spending on U.S. machines if rectangle I is larger than rectangle II. But it will always increase the French demand for dollars, as dollar spending on U.S. machines will rise by $10,000 × AB (the area of rectangle III).

A. The Supply and Demand for U.S. Exports: Prices in foreign currency (francs)

B. The Supply and Demand for U.S. Exports: Prices in domestic currency (dollars)

Consider, next, the impact of depreciation on the supply of dollars, analyzed in Fig. 4-2.[3] The vertical axis of this diagram measures the dollar price of French cars and the horizontal axis measures the number of cars imported by the United States. If, to start, the supply curve is G_1 and the demand curve is F_1, there will be an equilibrium at T_1. Americans will import OD cars. If, later, the dollar depreciates by 60 per cent (raising the price of the franc from $0.25 to $0.40), the dollar price of a French car will rise by 60 per cent, and the supply curve facing American buyers will shift to G_2. Equilibrium will be displaced to T_2, and the volume of imports will decline to OC.

[3] Here we do not need two panels, for Fig. 4-2 by itself will show us the change in dollar supply.

59

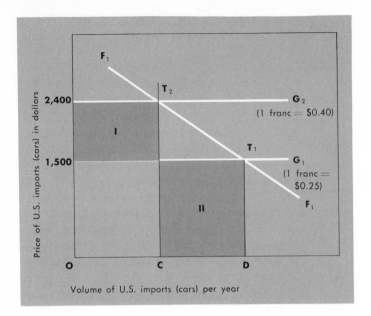

FIG. 4-2 Currency depreciation and the demand for imports. A depreciation of the dollar could raise or lower the supply of dollars on the foreign-exchange market. It will raise the supply if rectangle I is larger than rectangle II. It will lower the supply if rectangle I is smaller than rectangle II.

The change in American spending on French cars can be divided into two parts. Rectangle I in Fig. 4-2 shows the first part—the extra dollar outlay on cars bought after the depreciation. Rectangle II shows the second part—the decline in dollar outlay due to lower import volume. If rectangle I is smaller than rectangle II, a depreciation of the dollar will decrease the supply of dollars. If rectangle II is smaller than rectangle I, the depreciation will increase the supply.[4]

But even if depreciation raises the supply of dollars, it may still diminish the *excess supply*. The increase in demand for dollars, shown by Fig. 4-1, can exceed an increase in over-all supply, occurring when rectangle II is smaller than rectangle I in Fig. 4-2.[5] To see that this is so, look at Fig. 4-3. There, the vertical axis measures the price of the dollar in French francs, and the horizontal axis measures the number of dollars traded per year. The curve d_1 is a demand curve for dollars, derived from the French demand curve for U.S. exports. It shows what you have already discovered: that the demand for dollars will increase as the price of the dollar falls. The curve s_1 is a supply curve of dollars, derived from the U.S. demand curve for imports. It shows that the supply of dollars may move either way—that the amount supplied can actually increase as the price of the dollar falls. In a free market for foreign exchange, the point Z_1 would locate an equilibrium, and the exchange rate would settle at 4.0 francs to the dollar. If, however, the foreign demand

[4] In the economists' professional jargon, rectangle I will be larger, and the supply curve of dollars will be negatively sloped when plotted against the franc price of the dollar, if the American demand for imports is *price-inelastic;* it will be positively sloped if the American demand for imports is *price-elastic.*

[5] In professional jargon, depreciation will help to remove an excess supply of dollars in the foreign-exchange market if the sum of the *price-elasticities of demand and supply* is positive (if the supply curve cuts the demand curve from below).

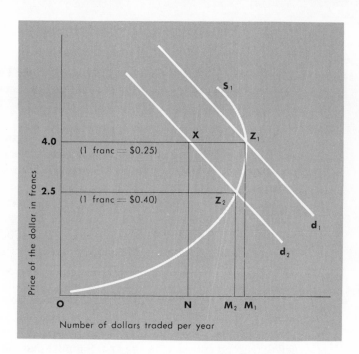

FIG. 4-3 Supply and demand in the foreign-exchange market. A decrease in the demand for dollars (the shift in the demand curve from d_1 to d_2) would cause the dollar to depreciate. Fewer francs would be needed to buy a dollar, and a dollar would buy fewer francs.

for U.S. exports were to fall, the foreign demand for dollars would also fall, shifting to d_2. At the old exchange rate, there would be an excess supply of dollars, Z_1X or NM_1 in the foreign-exchange market. The dollar would depreciate, raising the number of dollars demanded by NM_2 and lowering the number of dollars supplied by M_1M_2. A new equilibrium would take hold at Z_2 and the excess supply of dollars would disappear.

Payments Adjustment under a Pure Gold Standard

The old-fashioned gold standard furnished a simple way to maintain fixed exchange rates and to regulate the quantity of money. Under the gold standard, each government defined its monetary unit (the dollar, pound, franc, etc.) in grains or ounces of gold metal, then stood ready to sell gold for its currency and its currency for gold. Some governments went further, issuing gold coins, but this was not vital. The gold-standard mechanism worked as well when governments issued paper money fully backed by gold, so that any change in central-bank gold holdings forced an equal change in currency outstanding (or in bank reserves).

There are vestiges of this arrangement in the American monetary system. The United States Treasury still buys gold from foreign governments at $35 per Troy ounce (less a small commission) and sells it at that same price (plus a small commission). The dollar, then is valued at 1/35 of an ounce of gold. Furthermore, the Federal Reserve Banks must hold $25 in gold certificates for every $100 of Federal Reserve Notes outstanding. Those gold certificates give them title to Treasury gold. But the United States does not sell gold to individuals, here or abroad. Nor is there any direct link between

61

the U.S. gold stock and the supply of money in the United States. The Federal Reserve Banks can increase their liabilities (currency and bank reserves) by buying government securities in the open market, without also taking on more gold.

If all currencies were pegged to gold, and governments were willing to deal in gold with private citizens as well as with other governments, an *implicit* exchange rate would be established between each pair of currencies. If, for example, the French franc were freely exchangeable for gold at 140 francs per ounce of gold, it would exchange for $0.25 in American currency; 140 francs would buy an ounce of gold and an ounce of gold would buy $35. Hence, 140 francs = $35, and 1 franc = $35/140 = $0.25. The actual exchange rates could still fluctuate a bit, since governments might charge small commissions and bankers would have to pay the cost of shipping gold from one country to another. But when an exchange rate ran outside the boundaries set by these commissions and costs, someone could profit by engaging in *arbitrage*. He could buy gold with the currency that was at a discount in the foreign-exchange market, sell it for the currency that was at a premium, then sell the second currency for the first. Suppose that the franc rose from $0.25 to $0.28 and that it cost $0.10 in commissions and freight to ship an ounce of gold from New York to Paris. An *arbitrageur* could buy a thousand ounces of gold from the U.S. Treasury and ship them to Paris at a total cost of $35,100. He could sell the gold to the Bank of France for 140,000 francs, and then buy back dollars with the francs. As $0.28 \times 140,000 = $39,200, he would make a $4,100 profit on his capital, nearly 12 per cent, in a matter of days. He would also help to raise the price of the dollar, by exchanging francs for dollars at the end of his three-part transaction. Arbitrage would therefore serve to keep the actual exchange rate close to the ratio of gold parities.

How would these transactions show up in a supply-and-demand diagram of the foreign-exchange market (Fig. 4-3) and in the balance-of-payments statistics (Table 4-1)? With flexible exchange-rates, a shift in the demand for dollars was met by a change in the price of the dollar; when the demand curve in Fig. 4-3 dropped from d_1 to d_2, the exchange rate changed from 4.0 to 2.5 francs per U.S. dollar. With a pure gold standard, a shift in the demand curve would produce a gold flow, and this flow would keep the exchange rate from changing. A drop in the demand curve would cause an outflow of gold from the United States, equal to XZ_1 dollars per year. This gold loss would replace the excess supply of dollars in the foreign-exchange market. It would also show up as a *credit* item in the cash account of the balance of payments. The upper panel of Table 4-2 reproduces the cash account of Table 4-1, showing the $100,000 increase in foreign holdings of dollars and the $230,000 decrease in American holdings of foreign currency. The lower panel of Table 4-2 shows that same account after the banks have adjusted their working balances. The foreign banks have sold $50,000; the American banks have bought $130,000 worth of foreign currencies. The $180,000 worth of foreign currencies needed to finance these two changes are supplied by gold arbitrage. The third step in arbitrage (the exchange of francs for dollars) supplies $180,000 worth of francs to the foreign-exchange market and takes $180,000 of U.S. currency out of the market. The last line of Table 4-2 lists this gold arbitrage, showing a transfer of $180,000 worth of gold from the U.S. Treasury to the Bank of France.

Table 4-2 GOLD-MARKET ARBITRAGE AND THE CASH ACCOUNT IN THE U.S. BALANCE OF PAYMENTS (Thousands of dollars)

A. The Cash Account before Gold-Market Arbitrage

Private holdings:	+330
Increase (+) in foreign holdings of dollars	+100
Increase (−) in U.S. holdings of foreign currency	+230

B. The Cash Account after Gold-Market Arbitrage

Private holdings:	+150
Increase (+) in foreign holdings of dollars	+ 50
Increase (−) in U.S. holdings of foreign currency	+100
Official holdings:	+180
Increase (−) in U.S. gold stock	+180

Table 4-2 also offers us a second way to measure the U.S. payments deficit—by the change in official holdings of cash assets (gold and foreign currencies). We shall call this statistic the *net payments deficit,* or *deficit measured by official settlements,* and will use it from here on as the best available measure of payments disequilibrium. It is far better than the *gross deficit* because it corresponds to the notion of excess supply in the foreign-exchange market. Although there was a $330,000 gross deficit in Table 4-1, there was no pressure on the price of the dollar in the foreign-exchange market until the commercial banks tried to adjust their inventories of foreign currency. It was this adjustment that gave rise to an excess supply, causing the dollar to depreciate under flexible exchange rates. It was this same change in bank holdings that brought about arbitrage under the gold standard. And it will be this same change that brings about official intervention in the foreign-exchange market under a system of managed exchange rates.

The notion of *net deficit* has another virtue. It identifies the cash flows that trigger major changes in the deficit and surplus countries' money supplies. Under a pure gold standard, the country in *net deficit* will suffer a decline in its money supply, while the country in *net surplus* will experience an increase. These monetary changes are direct results of the gold movements that measure net deficits and surpluses. They are unavoidable under a gold standard, as the central banks cannot offset them by open-market operations. In consequence, a pure gold standard is guaranteed to combat disequilibria.

To trace the process of adjustment under the gold standard, look at

63

Table 4-3. The adjustment begins when a broker buys $180,000 worth of gold from the Treasury. The Treasury deposits the broker's check at the Federal Reserve Bank of New York, enlarging its balance there and replacing one monetary asset (gold) with another (a bank deposit). The Federal Reserve Bank sends the broker's check to the commercial bank on which it was drawn, and deducts $180,000 from that bank's deposit balance, reducing one of its deposit liabilities to offset the increase in another. The commercial bank can also balance its books. It deducts $180,000 from the broker's own account when the broker's check arrives, reducing its total liabilities to offset the decline in its assets.[6]

Table 4-3 GOLD FLOWS AND THE U.S. MONEY SUPPLY: CHANGES IN TREASURY, FEDERAL RESERVE AND COMMERCIAL-BANK BALANCE SHEETS (Thousands of dollars)

Institution and Item	Asset	Liability
U.S. Treasury		
Gold stock	−180	—
Balance at Federal Reserve Bank	+180	—
Federal Reserve Bank of New York		
Treasury deposit balance	—	+180
Member-bank deposit balance	—	−180
Commercial Bank		
Member-bank deposit balance	−180	—
Broker's deposit balance	—	−180

When these transactions are complete, everyone has balanced books. But the process of monetary contraction is far from finished. If the commercial banks were "loaned up" before the gold loss (if they had no excess reserves), they must now cut down their lending and deposits. Suppose they must maintain a 10 per cent reserve against demand deposits. They will have to reduce their deposit obligations by a full $1,800,000, because they have lost $180,000 in reserve balances. To do so, they must cut back their loans or investments by $1,620,000. When this process (summarized in Table 4-4) is completed, the $180,000 gold loss will have reduced the money supply by $1,800,000.

Similar transactions would occur in France, but running the other way. When the broker sold his gold to the Bank of France, he would receive a check drawn on the Bank of France. He must sell that check to move back into dollars, but the foreign-exchange dealer buying it from him would, in turn, deposit it with a French commercial bank. That bank would send the

---

[6] The chain of transactions may not end at this point. The Treasury may use its extra cash balance to retire gold certificates held by the Federal Reserve Bank, for it no longer has the gold that "backed" those certificates. But this additional transaction occurs within the government; it does not affect the commercial banks or the money supply.

check back to the Bank of France and would receive extra reserves. French banks would be able to expand their lending and the French money supply.

Monetary changes such as these would change interest rates in the United States and France, affecting the current and capital accounts. A decrease in the U.S. money supply would raise U.S. interest rates; an increase in the French money supply would reduce French interest rates. Short-term capital would flow to the United States in search of higher yields, augmenting the demand for dollars in the foreign-exchange market. Domestic spending would decline in the United States and would rise in France, causing wage and price changes that would have the same effects as an exchange-rate change.

Table 4-4 GOLD FLOWS AND THE U.S. MONEY SUPPLY:
MEMORANDUM ON COMMERCIAL-BANK RESERVES (Thousands of dollars)

Initial decrease in deposit liabilities		180
Decrease in total reserves (member-bank balances)	180	
Decrease in required reserves (10 per cent reserve requirement against demand deposits)	18	
Reserve deficiency	162	
Secondary decrease in lending and deposits (due to deficiency)		1,620
Total decrease in deposit liabilities		1,800

Interest rates and capital movements. An increase in U.S. interest rates relative to foreign rates can generate several types of short-term lending and investment. First, it may alter the financing of foreign trade. An American importer who usually borrows dollars from a New York bank and converts them to sterling to pay for British goods may, instead, borrow sterling directly from a London bank. A British importer who ordinarily borrows dollars in New York may, instead, borrow sterling in London, then swap it for dollars to pay for his purchases. American importers who borrow in London reduce the supply of dollars in the exchange market. British importers who borrow in London increase the demand for dollars. Hence, changes in the *locus* of commercial borrowing will help to reduce the excess supply of dollars. Next, a change in interest rates can foster explicit cash transfers. A British corporation that normally invests its idle funds in British Treasury bills may send its money to New York to buy U.S. Treasury bills or other money-market instruments. An American corporation that normally holds money in London to finance its foreign operations may transfer cash to New York to earn a higher interest rate. These two transfers will also increase the demand for dollars.

But short-term capital flows can only aid the dollar temporarily; money borrowed today must be repaid in a few months. Furthermore, there is a built-in market mechanism working to arrest transfers of funds. When American importers borrow in London and British firms place cash in New York, they run the risk that the dollar will depreciate. Were this to happen, Americans would have to spend more dollars to repay their sterling debts, and

British companies would get fewer pounds for the dollars they invested in New York.[7] To protect themselves against this exchange risk, investors and borrowers can arrange *forward* foreign-exchange contracts. They can promise to deliver dollars for pounds at some future date but at an exchange rate fixed by the contracts. But the *forward exchange rates* at which such contracts can be made may be quite different from the *spot rates* at which currencies are traded for immediate delivery. Investors may therefore incur extra costs. Furthermore, the forward dollar-sterling rate will tend to move in sympathy with the interest-rate difference, offsetting the incentive to borrow in London or invest in New York. When interest rates are higher in New York than in London, the pound tends toward a premium in the forward market (see Fig. 4-4). This is because importers borrowing in London and companies investing in New York are buying forward sterling to *hedge* against exchange risks and thereby augmenting the demand for forward sterling.

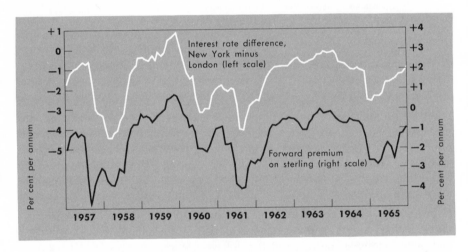

FIG. 4-4 Differences in short-term rates and the premium on forward foreign exchange. When New York interest rates are above London interest rates, the pound rises to a premium in the forward foreign-exchange market. When London interest rates are above New York rates, the pound falls to a discount. The relationship is even closer than the chart indicates; the right scale has been lowered to disentangle the two lines. (Source: Board of Governors of the Federal Reserve System, *Federal Reserve Bulletin*, various issues.)

To sum up, an interest-rate difference caused by changes in money supplies can help to remove a payments deficit, but can rarely do the whole job. A more lasting change is needed to remove an excess supply of dollars. The gold standard has also to alter costs and prices.

Interest rates, spending, and prices. Early economic theory connected

[7] This risk is much greater with managed exchange rates than with a pure gold standard. But it also existed in the heyday of the gold standard, before 1914. Exchange rates could still move within the so-called "gold points," and gold parities could change.

money and prices by a simple axiom: If the supply of money falls, prices have to fall, so that the remaining currency can do its work efficiently. Early writers on international finance consequently argued that a gold standard would be self-adjusting. A gold transfer from Britain to France would reduce British prices and raise French prices; the citizens of both countries would buy more British goods and fewer French goods; Britain would develop a surplus on current account; gold would flow back to Britain. David Hume, the eighteenth-century philosopher, put this *specie-flow doctrine* very neatly:

> Suppose four-fifths of all the money in Great Britain to be annihilated in one night, and the nation reduced to the same condition, with regard to specie, as in the reigns of the Harrys and Edwards, what would be the consequence? Must not the price of all labour and commodities sink in proportion, and everything be sold as cheap as they were in those ages? What nation could then dispute with us in any foreign market, or pretend to navigate or to sell manufacturers at the same price, which to us would afford sufficient profit? In how little time, therefore, must this bring back the money which we had lost, and raise us to the level of all the neighboring nations? Where, after we have arrived, we immediately lose the advantage of the cheapness of labour and commodities; and the farther flowing in of money is stopped by our fulness and repletion.

But even if wages and prices moved smoothly, the connection between money and prices would be less direct than Hume implied. Most economists would first link the supply of money to the rate of interest, then link the interest rate to total spending, spending to employment, and employment to wage rates. Only then would they come to prices.

A fall in the quantity of money will increase the interest rate because it is accomplished by reductions in bank lending—in the supply of loanable funds—and a cut in the supply of credit will raise its price. When interest rates increase, however, aggregate spending is apt to fall. Some forms of business investment are sensitive to changes in interest rates or to the credit rationing that comes with higher interest rates. Reductions in investment, moreover, depress every form of private spending; a *multiplier* process is set to work, reducing consumption along with investment. Finally, a reduction in aggregate spending will depress output and employment, and the consequent increase in unemployment will cause workers to bid down money wage rates, cutting costs and prices.

From here on, the argument is much like Hume's own exposition, with one qualification. A reduction in the prices of the country losing gold relative to those of the country gaining gold will increase the exports of the deficit country and reduce its imports. This will improve its balance of payments and stem its gold loss, provided the changes in the volume of trade are larger than the changes in prices. But just as one expects exchange depreciation to improve a country's balance of payments, so one would expect deflation to **67** do so. The gold-standard mechanism and exchange-rate changes have similar effects if wage rates are flexible. The chief difference between them is that an exchange-rate change moves one vital price, whereas the gold standard keeps that one price constant and moves all the rest.

Payments Adjustment under Managed Exchange Rates

Although the United States pegs its currency to gold, we do not have a pure gold standard. As the Federal Reserve Banks can hold other assets (government securities) against their liabilities (currency and member-bank deposits), there is no strict link between gold movements and the American money supply. Furthermore, other currencies are not pegged to gold, so that there is no implicit exchange rate between the dollar and those currencies. Yet most countries do maintain stable exchange rates by direct action. Instead of holding gold as "backing" for their currencies and passively awaiting gold-market arbitrage, they have established exchange stabilization funds under central bank or treasury control. These funds hold gold and foreign currencies and use these reserves to finance intervention in the foreign-exchange markets. When the price of a country's currency rises, its exchange stabilization fund sells domestic currency for foreign currencies, reducing the price. It adds the foreign currencies to its portfolio. When the price of the domestic currency falls, the exchange stabilization fund buys that currency with foreign currencies, raising the price. It takes the foreign currency out of its reserves. In Fig. 4-3, for example, the Bank of France might buy up Z_1X dollars, the excess supply, to keep the exchange rate stable at four francs to the dollar. It would put French francs into the market and take out dollars. The Bank of France could retain the dollars it had bought, or could convert them into gold at the U.S. Treasury.[8] The Bank of France need not act as soon as the exchange rate starts to change, but under the rules of the International Monetary Fund, it must intervene whenever the exchange rate moves by as much as 1 per cent from its established parity. This 1 per cent margin is akin to the range that existed under the gold standard.

If the Bank of France decides to buy gold with the dollars taken from the foreign-exchange market, the U.S. cash account will look just as it did under the gold standard (Table 4-2). If it holds onto the dollars, the numbers in the cash account will be the same as they were in Table 4-2, but the last line will read "Increase (+) in foreign official holdings of dollars."

If the Bank of France does buy gold, the American money supply will

---

[8] Thus, the size of U.S. gold losses depends on the size of the U.S. payments deficit *and* on the reserve-asset preferences of foreign central banks. If the United States runs a payments deficit *vis-à-vis* countries whose central banks usually hold onto the dollars they acquire, the U.S. payments deficit need not cause a gold loss. If it runs a deficit *vis-à-vis* countries whose central banks normally hold gold, like Britain, France, and Switzerland, it will almost always lose some gold. The United States can also lose gold without having a deficit. This may happen when a dollar-holding country runs a deficit with a gold-holding country, transferring dollar deposits to a central bank that will use them to buy gold. It can also lose gold when a foreign central bank alters its portfolio of reserve assets. One such instance occurred in 1964-1965, when France cashed in $1 billion of dollar reserves.

begin to fall, as it did in Tables 4-3 and 4-4. If it holds onto the dollars, there may still be a decline in the money supply, but the process will differ from that of the gold standard. Many central banks keep their dollars on deposit with the Federal Reserve Banks. To do so, the Bank of France will draw a check on the New York commercial bank where its dollars lay when it acquired them from a foreign-exchange dealer. It will send that check to the Federal Reserve Bank of New York, which will credit the Bank of France with $180,000 and deduct the same amount from the deposit account of the commercial bank. The commercial bank's reserves will fall by $180,000, and it will have to cut back its loans or investments. There will also be an increase in the French money supply. When the Bank of France buys dollars from the foreign-exchange market, it creates new French francs, and these will find their way into the reserves of the French commercial banks.

Table 4-5 U.S. GOLD STOCK AND COMMERCIAL-BANK
RESERVE BALANCES AT THE FEDERAL RESERVE BANKS
(Millions of dollars)

Item	1939-1941	1961-1963
Change in U.S. gold stock	+5,241	−4,367
Change in foreign deposits at the Federal Reserve Banks	+ 792 *	− 69
Net foreign influence (gold *less* deposits)	+4,449	−4,298
Federal Reserve credit, currency in circulation, and Treasury operations	−3,108	+4,342
Total (equals change in commercial-bank reserve balances at the Federal Reserve Banks)	+1,341	+ 44

* Includes the change in "other" domestic deposits which could not be separated from foreign accounts.

Source: Board of Governors of the Federal Reserve System, *Federal Reserve Bulletin.*

If this were all that happened under managed exchange rates, the system would resemble a pure-gold standard. There would be an increase in U.S. interest rates and a drop in French rates. Short-term capital would flow to the United States and prices would begin to change, altering trade flows and stemming the deficit. But something else can happen with managed exchange rates. The central banks may not allow money stocks to change. The Federal Reserve Banks may buy government securities in the open market to replenish American bank reserves, forestalling a contraction in loans and deposits. The Bank of France may sell government securities to reduce French bank reserves, forestalling an increase in loans and deposits.[9]

Central banks are very apt to follow these policies—to "neutralize" gold flows. Look at Table 4-5 to see two such episodes. In 1939-1941, the

[9] Central banks can also change the reserve requirements under which the commercial banks operate. The Federal Reserve System can reduce the U.S. reserve ratio; the Bank of France can raise the French reserve ratio. They can thereby align reserve requirements with the actual changes in reserves.

U.S. gold stock rose by $5.2 billion. Part of this increase was allowed to augment bank reserves, but most of it was offset by open-market operations. In 1961-1963, the U.S. gold stock fell by $4.4 billion, but the entire change was offset by domestic operations.

DOMESTIC AND EXTERNAL EQUILIBRIUM

Why should central banks offset external disturbances when, by doing so, they interfere with the restoration of payments equilibrium? Why have the Federal Reserve Banks neutralized U.S. gold losses in the 1960's, allowing the United States to go on running a payments deficit?

The answer is quite simple. To achieve an external equilibrium by domestic deflation is very much more painful than we have indicated heretofore. Wage rates and prices do not fall easily, and a decline in total spending brought about by higher interest rates (or by fiscal policy) will lead to unemployment, not to wage reductions. If the United States sought to reach external balance by following the gold-standard rules, it would have to sacrifice full employment. Its imports would still shrink as domestic spending fell. But the decline in its imports would be caused by a reduction in its real income, not by a reduction in prices. Furthermore, a balance-of-payments deficit can sometimes depress employment directly, and governments are loath to compound this direct effect. They may even try to combat it.

National Income and Foreign Trade

To understand the links between exports, imports, and employment when wages are rigid, you must start with the basic income identities.[10] In an open economy (one with foreign trade), three types of spending contribute to the national income:

C Consumption (household spending)
I Investment (business spending)
X Exports (foreign spending)

But each of these three streams includes spending on imported goods as well as domestic products; even exports may include imported raw materials. One must therefore deduct imports, M, from total spending in order to define domestic income, Y:

$$C+I+X-M=Y$$

This accounting relationship tells only half the story. To complete it, one has now to note that some of the spending streams listed in the basic income equation are themselves affected by the levels of income.

[10] This analysis ignores the role of government expenditure, as its inclusion would complicate the analysis without changing the result.

Consumption, exports, and imports depend quite directly on national income. Given an extra dollar of income, consumers will usually spend part of it on goods and services. This connection is a basic building block of economic analysis. Imports and exports depend on prices and exchange rates, but also respond to changes in income. Imports will increase along with income at home. Exports will increase with income abroad (being the imports of other countries). If, indeed, prices and exchange rates are stable, the connection between income and imports will be much like the link between income and consumption. Part of any increase in income will be spent on imports.[11]

The remaining component of income, business investment, depends on many things, and income may be one of them. But we will suppose that investment is governed by the rate of interest—that it will rise when interest rates fall, and will fall when interest rates rise. On this assumption, monetary policy will affect national income by affecting investment.

The two-way relationship between trade and income gives rise to an important balancing mechanism. Suppose that a change in foreign tastes causes a decline in exports. This decline will produce a payments deficit, but will also cut back national income. The reduction in income will then reduce spending on imports, narrowing the payments deficit. And income will fall more than exports because the decline in income will include a decline in consumption. Hence, the reduction in imports may be quite large.

But the decrease in imports induced by this process may not be large enough to match the drop in exports; there may still be a payments deficit when income and imports have ceased to change. This is because consumers will cut back their savings when they experience reductions in income, and a change in savings will short-circuit the process of payments adjustment. Define savings, S, as the difference between income, Y, and consumption, C, and subtract C from both sides of the accounting relationship given above:

$$I+X-M=Y-C=S$$

It follows that:

$$X-M=S-I$$

[11] Actually, the income-import link may be a percentage relationship, rather than a fractional (linear) relationship; in the professional jargon, the *marginal propensity to import* may not be constant, but the *income-elasticity of demand for imports* may be nearly constant. As evidence, look at the percentage changes in imports and gross national product during two recent cyclical upturns in the United States:

	Imports	G.N.P.
First quarter 1958 to second quarter 1959	+22.9	+12.7
First quarter 1961 to second quarter 1962	+19.7	+10.2

The ratio of the change in imports to the change in G.N.P. (the *income-elasticity of demand for imports*) works out at 1.8 in the first upturn and 1.9 in the second upturn. These figures, however, may be a shade higher than the long-run income-elasticity because they refer to cyclical swings and include a large amount of inventory investment in imported products. **71**

Exports and imports cannot be equal unless savings and investment are also equal. Nor can exports and imports change by like amounts unless savings and investment change by like amounts (or fail to change at all). When, then, savings fall as income falls, the reduction in exports responsible for the drop in income will exceed the reduction in imports caused by the drop in income.

This same argument is traced out arithmetically in Section A of Table 4-6. There, an autonomous decline in exports by 100 causes income to decline by 250 and cuts savings and imports by 50 each. Taken together, savings and imports combined have fallen by as much as exports. But because savings have changed with income, imports have not fallen far enough to close the trade-balance gap. In order to re-establish payments equilibrium, the government must foster a further reduction in national income. It must let the payments deficit cut into the supply of money, and may even have to hasten the contraction by open-market operations; it must end the deficit before it has eaten up the country's reserves of gold and foreign exchange. As monetary

Table 4-6 CHANGES IN INCOME AND ITS COMPONENTS
DUE TO A DECLINE IN EXPORTS (The marginal propensity
to consume is 0.8; the marginal propensity to import is 0.2.)

Period	Income from Last Period (1)	Consump- tion (2)	Savings (3)	Invest- ment (4)	Exports (5)	Imports (6)	Current Income (7)	Trade Balance (8)
Section A. An autonomous decrease in exports								
1	0	0	0	0	−100.0	0	−100.0	−100.0
2	−100.0	− 80.0	− 20.0	0	−100.0	− 20.0	−160.0	− 80.0
3	−160.0	−128.0	− 32.0	0	−100.0	− 32.0	−196.0	− 68.0
4	−196.0	−156.8	− 39.2	0	−100.0	− 39.2	−217.6	− 60.8
—	—	—	—	—	—	—	—	—
—	—	—	—	—	—	—	—	—
Final	−250.0	−200.0	− 50.0	0	−100.0	− 50.0	−250.0	− 50.0
Section B. A decrease in investment induced by higher interest rates								
1	−250.0	−200.0	− 50.0	−100.0	−100.0	− 50.0	−350.0	− 50.0
2	−350.0	−280.0	− 70.0	−100.0	−100.0	− 70.0	−410.0	− 30.0
3	−410.0	−328.0	− 82.0	−100.0	−100.0	− 82.0	−446.0	− 18.0
4	−446.0	−356.8	− 89.2	−100.0	−100.0	− 89.2	−467.6	− 10.8
—	—	—	—	—	—	—	—	—
—	—	—	—	—	—	—	—	—
Final	−500.0	−400.0	−100.0	−100.0	−100.0	−100.0	−500.0	0

Explanation of Entries:
(1) Income of the previous period carried over from column 7.
(2) Four-fifths of the entry in column 1.
(3) Income less consumption (1 − 2).
(4) An independent variable; there is no change in investment at the first stage, then a 100 drop due to an increase in interest rates.
(5) An independent variable; there is a 100 drop at the start.
(6) One-fifth of the entry in column 1.
(7) The sum of current consumption, investment, and exports less imports (2 + 4 + 5 − 6).
(8) Current exports *less* current imports (5 − 6).

contraction will raise interest rates, it will depress domestic investment, reducing income and imports. This process is traced out in Section B of Table 4-6 where, in the end, savings, investment, exports, and imports have all fallen by 100.

But payments equilibrium can only be restored at considerable cost. There have been two doses of deflation in this example (the initial cut in exports and the later cut in domestic investment), so that income has dedeclined by 500, generating unemployment. Furthermore, a reduction in one country's imports will reduce some other country's income; deflation in one country is apt to spread to others by way of foreign trade.

To sum up, rigid wages make deflation a painful way to maintain external balance, and governments are often tempted to offset the automatic monetary processes, rather than to reinforce them. Faced with a conflict between policy objectives—the need to maintain payments equilibrium and to foster full employment—they are apt to favor domestic goals for as long as possible. In the 1930's, for example, many countries facing payments deficits resorted to tariffs, quotas, and exchange controls to avoid a further increase in unemployment. More recently, a number of governments have faced the same dilemma, including the United States and Great Britain, and have imposed a variety of subtle trade restrictions so as to avoid deflationary measures.

Adjustment Amidst Economic Growth

The process of adjustment under fixed exchange rates would not be so painful if wage rates were flexible. Nor will it be so painful when adjustment is imbedded in global economic growth. A growing economy can alter its costs even though its wage rates are rigid. It can also alter national expenditure without creating massive unemployment. It can seek to tamper with the rates of increase in wages and expenditure, not with the absolute levels.

Suppose, first, that labor productivity is rising steadily in all countries. If a deficit country can hold its wage rates constant, while foreign wages rise apace with productivity, costs and prices will decline in the deficit country, and its balance of payments will improve without any absolute loss of output or employment.

Suppose, next, that output and money incomes are growing together in all countries, so that prices do not change. If a deficit country can keep its domestic expenditure from rising apace with output, it will be able to hold down its imports and enlarge its export capacity. It will experience a gradual improvement in its balance of payments.

But these growth effects are more easily described than achieved. And while they have a cumulative impact, they work very slowly. Payments deficits and surpluses may therefore endure for quite a while, straining international financial arrangements. Even under favorable circumstances, the maintenance of payments equilibrium will remain a difficult policy problem.

73

SUMMARY

Foreign economic policy has two major dimensions. An open economy must formulate *commercial* policies to reap the gains from foreign trade and foreign investment. It must formulate *financial* policies to maintain a monetary equilibrium in its foreign transactions.

The choice among exchange-rate regimes is the first step in making international financial policy. With exchange rates free to fluctuate as market forces dictate, a difference between foreign payments and receipts will appear as excess supply or demand in the foreign-exchange market. An excess supply of domestic currency will cause its price to decline (depreciate); an excess demand will cause it to increase (appreciate). A change in the exchange rate will alter the foreign prices of a country's exports and the domestic prices of its imports. It will have the same effect as a change in a country's over-all price level. A depreciation or deflation will increase the foreign and domestic demand for home goods (shifting demand away from foreign goods) and will restore equilibrium in the foreign-exchange market.

With exchange rates fixed by a gold standard or official intervention in the foreign-exchange markets, an excess supply of home currency will cause a contraction in the domestic money supply and a corresponding expansion abroad. These monetary changes will also re-establish equilibrium, though differently from flexible exchange-rates. They will raise interest rates in the deficit country and depress them in the surplus country. These changes in interest rates will call forth capital flows and will cause price changes affecting the current account.

With rigid costs and prices, however, adjustment must take place through income changes. Some of these changes will occur automatically; a decrease in exports will reduce national income, cutting domestic expenditure on home goods and imports. Some of the changes are indirect, brought on by monetary policy. Higher interest rates in a deficit country will depress investment, reducing income and imports. These indirect effects will continue to operate until the deficit is ended. The money supply will go on shrinking, interest rates will go on rising, and investment will continue to fall, reducing income and imports. With fixed exchange-rates and rigid wage-rates, however, governments may face an intractable policy conflict. They may have to choose between full employment and payments equilibrium.

THE CHOICE AMONG
EXCHANGE-RATE REGIMES

The world's monetary system most nearly resembled a gold standard during the 40 years before the First World War. By the mid-1870's, each major country had connected its currency to gold, establishing a system of fixed exchange rates which was not altered until 1914. And after the completion of the Atlantic Cable, linking London and New York, the market exchange rates stayed close to their gold parities.

Governments did not give up all of their control over the supply of money. They did not base their currencies wholly on gold. In the United States, for example, banks could issue paper money backed by holdings of government securities. In Britain, the Bank of England bought and sold commercial bills and government securities to ease or tighten credit. But Britain and some other countries adhered to the "rules of the game"; they used monetary policy to reinforce rather than offset the impact of gold flows.

Yet the international payments system did not work quite as theory said it should. The major countries sometimes corrected their payments positions by altering output and employment rather than prices. They sometimes shifted the burden of adjustment onto countries at the periphery of the world economy—the raw-materials producers of the Western Hemisphere and other outlying areas. A tightening of credit in Britain bore heavily on trade in

75

raw materials because this trade was financed with money lent by London. When British interest rates were high and credit scarce in London, dealers in raw materials had to compress their inventories. Doing so, they depressed the prices of raw materials and reduced Britain's import bill. The countries at the periphery, moreover, changed their exchange rates rather often, dropping away from the gold standard during payments crises, and returning at different gold parities.

After the First World War had wrecked the monetary system, the statesmen tried to build a new gold standard. Unfortunately, this attempt ignored the major differences between pre-war theory and pre-war practice and was therefore doomed to fail. But it might have failed even if its builders had understood the pre-war system, for the economic environment had changed. First, there was less flexibility in the international economy—you have already read of the growth in debts, the increase in tariffs, the wide use of quotas, and the huge expansion in farm output. Second, there was less strength at the center of the international financial system—Britain's chief exports, textiles and coal, were meeting fierce competition in foreign markets, while New York and Paris had become major purveyors of capital and credit, so that London could no longer influence international credit conditions as it had before the war. Third, there was less tolerance of unemployment—new political parties drawing support from urban workers threatened any government that dared to cure its payments problems by deflation. Governments, moreover, had found new ways to insulate the national economy from international monetary changes. New central banks had been established in several countries, including the Federal Reserve System in the United States, and all central banks had found new ways to contravene the "rules of the game." Finally, the composition of international reserves had changed. Many countries were holding dollars and sterling, as well as gold. Sterling was the more important of the new reserve-assets; some countries, indeed, invested the bulk of their reserves in London. Even the Bank of France, a pillar of monetary orthodoxy, built up large sterling claims in the 1920's. The new system, then, was a *gold-exchange standard,* not a simple gold standard.

This substitution of currencies for gold was, in part, inspired by fears of a gold shortage and was sanctioned by international financial conferences. But it proved to be a major weakness. Britain had become a banker to other governments and was continually threatened by a run on its own small gold reserves—just like any other banker with no central bank to serve him as lender of last resort. The run finally came in 1931, and dealt the new system its death blow. In 1925, Britain had pegged the pound at its old gold parity, taking no account of the increase in British prices or the weakness of Britain's export industries. As a result, the United States and France ran very large payments surpluses. The United States succeeded in masking its surplus by heavy long-term lending to other countries—huge private purchases of newly issued foreign bonds. France took in gold and built up its sterling claims. With the collapse of the American economy, however, American lending came to a halt. In 1928 there had been a net capital outflow of $1,541,000,000. In 1931 there was a net *inflow* of $756,000,000, and new U.S. purchases of foreign securities were not even large enough to cover redemptions, let alone the massive repatriation of other American capital. At this same critical moment, moreover, the Bank of France began to convert its sterling into gold, putting heavy pressure on the pound. Britain was compelled to abandon the new gold standard in the summer of 1931, when a panic that had started with the collapse of the *Credit Anstalt,* the Rothschild bank in Vienna, spread across Europe and began to lap at Britain's gold reserves.

The 1930's saw complete monetary chaos. Many small countries had left the gold standard in 1929 and 1930; others followed in 1931 and 1932. Their currencies fluctuated in the exchange market, propelled by underlying economic changes and by waves of speculation. Then the United States devalued the dollar; it left the gold standard in 1933 and came back to gold at a lower parity in 1934. The countries that had stayed with gold, including France and Italy, imposed new trade barriers to protect themselves against the competition of countries that had quit the gold standard and allowed their currencies to depreciate. Some governments went further, seeking to generate export surpluses and increase employment at the expense of their neighbors. The situation was not brought under control until 1936, when France and other gold-bloc countries changed their gold parities and arranged a "standstill" agreement with Britain and the United States, barring a new round of competitive depreciations. When the exchange rates had finally settled down, they were not much different from what they had been before 1931. Here are the percentage depreciations ($-$) in key currencies, based on 1930 exchange rates with the U.S. dollar:

	1932	1934	1936
United Kingdom	−33	+ 2	+ 1
India	−32	+ 2	+ 1
Australia	−41	−12	−13
Canada	−13	+ 1	0
Italy	0	+62	0
Belgium	0	+68	+21
France	0	+68	+19

The Commonwealth countries (India, Australia, and Canada) moved with Great Britain; their currencies depreciated through 1932 (for Britain had left gold in 1931), but strengthened in relation to the dollar by 1934 (for the dollar left gold in 1933). The gold-bloc countries, by contrast, showed no change until 1934, when the drop in the gold price of the dollar raised the dollar price of their currencies. By 1936, however, much of this premium had vanished; the gold-bloc countries had changed their own gold parities.

77

Summing up the 1920's and 1930's, one observer drew these conclusions:

> The twenty years between the wars have furnished ample evidence concerning the question of fluctuating *versus* stable exchanges. A system of completely free and flexible exchange rates is conceivable and may have certain attractions in theory.... Yet nothing would be more at variance with the lessons of the past.... In the first place, they create an element of risk which tends to discourage international trade.... Secondly, as a means of adjusting the balance of payments, exchange fluctuations involve constant shifts of labour and other resources between production for the home market and production for export.... Thirdly, experience has shown that ... any considerable or continuous movement of the exchange rate is liable to generate anticipations of a further movement in the same direction, thus giving rise to speculative capital transfers of a disequilibrating kind....[1]

This view had an enormous impact on the monetary system which rose from the wreckage of the Second World War.

The Bretton Woods System

This time, the governments avoided one of the grave errors they had committed after the First World War. They tried to deal separately with the needs of post-war reconstruction, rather than burdening the international monetary system with a new layer of indebtedness and straining the new system of exchange rates with abnormal import needs. The U.S. Lend-Lease program gave outright aid to America's allies in order to forestall the accumulation of new intergovernmental debts. A large U.S. loan to Britain in 1945 and the Marshall Plan of 1948 sought to finance reconstruction without drawing off the gold reserves of the war-shattered countries or saddling them with huge short-term obligations.

Governments likewise sought to work out new exchange rates by general agreement and to keep them stable once they had been fixed. They did not foreswear all exchange-rate changes, preferring devaluation [2] to exchange controls, trade controls, or deflation. Devaluation was preferred to exchange or trade controls because it does not distort resource allocation; it increases the foreign demand for domestic goods in addition to limiting the domestic demand for foreign goods. Import controls, by contrast, increase the domestic price of import-competing products, attracting domestic resources away from the more efficient export industries. Devaluation was preferred to deflation because it does not depress employment or halt economic growth. In modern

---

[1] Ragnar Nurkse, *International Currency Experience* (Geneva: League of Nations, 1944), pp. 210-211.

[2] We shall henceforth use the term *devaluation* when we mean a once-over change in a fixed exchange rate (accomplished by changing its gold parity or the price at which the central bank intervenes in the foreign-exchange market). We shall use the term *depreciation* when we mean a change in a flexible exchange-rate (accomplished by the market forces of supply and demand).

economies with wage and price rigidity, deflation leads to unemployment before it lowers prices. And every major government is pledged to maintain maximum employment and foster rapid growth.

The new exchange-rate system was enshrined in the Bretton Woods Agreement of 1944, which established the International Monetary Fund (IMF) and erected the framework for post-war monetary cooperation. Governments agreed to peg their currencies to gold or the U.S. dollar (which, in turn, is pegged to gold). They agreed to make their currencies convertible— to dismantle their exchange controls—after a transition period. And they agreed on rules to police exchange-rate changes. A government may alter the par value of its currency by as much as 10 per cent without IMF approval, but needs the Fund's approval for any larger change. This approval, moreover, will only be forthcoming when a country faces a "fundamental disequilibrium" in its international accounts.

The Bretton Woods system, sometimes called the system of the *adjustable peg,* seeks to assure maximum exchange-rate stability, yet to facilitate orderly changes when they are needed and to avoid competitive devaluations like those of the 1930's. There have been a number of important exchange-rate changes under the Bretton Woods system. In 1949, for example, Britain devalued the pound from $4.03 to $2.80, and was followed by many other countries in Europe and the Commonwealth. France devalued the franc in 1957. Germany and the Netherlands raised their parities in 1961. And India devalued the rupee in 1966. Exchange-rate changes have been particularly frequent in the less-developed countries—especially those of Latin America—just as they were in the nineteenth century. The less-developed countries have had difficulty maintaining price stability while seeking to promote more rapid growth; they lack the wide range of policy instruments available to countries with well-articulated money markets and fiscal systems, and have been afflicted by wide fluctuations in the prices of their major export products. In consequence, they have encountered serious balance-of-payments problems.

The Case for Greater Flexibility

Nevertheless, a growing number of economists argue that the Bretton Woods regime combines the disadvantages of fully fixed exchange rates with the disadvantage of flexible exchange rates.

First, they say, the Bretton Woods system encourages countries to employ undesirable methods of payments adjustment. Because the system treats a change in the exchange rate as the remedy of last resort, such a change becomes conspicuous rather than an everyday occurrence. Hence governments hesitate to alter their exchange rates; they tend to regard devaluation as a confession of failure. Some governments still resort to trade controls, overt or covert, distorting resource allocation. Others keep a tight rein on domestic demand, using restrictive monetary and fiscal policies; they forego economic growth to maintain payments equilibrium. This has been a common criticism of British policy and, at times, of American policy as well. More generally, critics say, the present system imparts a deflationary bias to the whole process of payments adjustment. A country that runs a payments deficit will eventually use up its reserves. But a surplus country can accumulate reserves indefinitely.[3] A deficit country may therefore be obliged to deflate or devalue its currency, while a surplus country cannot be compelled to inflate or appreciate. Under flexible exchange rates, by contrast, the market operates with an even hand, raising the price of the surplus country's currency and lowering the price of the deficit country's currency.

Critics also accuse the present system of fostering perverse capital movements that aggravate the basic payments problems. Speculation can be *destabilizing*. This is because traders and investors can "attack" a weak currency at negligible cost. Suppose that the price of the pound has fallen from $2.80 to $2.78, as far as it can with its present parity, and that Britain's reserves are slipping away as the Bank of England uses them to support the exchange rate. Speculators know that Britain cannot lose reserves forever, and they may begin to gamble on the possibility that Britain will devalue the pound. Some will sell the sterling securities they hold; others will borrow in London rather than abroad, hoping to repay their debts with cheaper pounds. These flows and others will add to the pressure on the price of the pound and force the Bank of England to use up even more reserves. If devaluation was possible before the speculation began, it can become nearly certain once speculation is underway.

If Britain does devalue the pound, the speculators will reap handsome profits. If the pound is not devalued, they can "unwind" their positions with very little loss; they will be able to buy the pounds they need at a slight additional cost. At worst, the pound will rise to its upper limit, $2.82, exacting a 4¢ premium from speculators when they come to rebuild their sterling holdings and pay off their sterling debts. But 4¢ on $2.80 is a mere 1.4 per cent—hardly a high price to pay for the chance of gaining 20 or 30 per cent from a devaluation.

Speculators can also attack a weak currency under a system of flexible exchange rates. But speculation would be much more costly, for the price of the pound could rise without limit, compelling the speculators to "unwind" their positions at a huge premium. Furthermore, some experts say, a system

[3] A surplus country may have difficulty offsetting the monetary impact of its payments surplus. To sop up the commercial-bank reserves created by a surplus, the central bank must engage in open-market sales of government securities or must raise commercial-bank reserve requirements. But it can run out of government securities. And by increasing reserve requirements, it ties up the assets of the commercial banks, diminishing bank profits. These things were happening in Germany in 1958-1961, when Germany experienced a massive payments surplus, the counterpart of the U.S. deficit, discussed below. They have led some Europeans to argue that the present system is inflationary, not deflationary, and to charge that Europe has had to "import inflation" from deficit countries, notably the United States.

of flexible exchange rates would actually engender *stabilizing* speculation, rather than *destabilizing* speculation. The activities of speculators would strengthen a weak currency rather than weaken it further.

The debate on this point has grown quite complex. But the basic point at issue is very simple. The advocates of flexible exchange rates argue that a drop in the price of any asset will attract more buyers, not more sellers. When a currency weakens in the foreign-exchange market, speculators will come to regard it as a bargain and will start to buy it. Doing so, they will arrest the decline in its price, and may even cause its price to rise. Likewise, as a currency appreciates, speculators will come to believe that it is priced too high and will start to sell it. Doing so, they will arrest or reverse the rise in price. If these propositions are true, speculation will dampen exchange-rate fluctuations, not amplify them.

This analysis of speculation builds on an implicit supposition that there is a trendless "normal" rate to guide the speculators when they make their judgments about future exchange rates. If there were no "normal" rate (or if it had a trend), speculators could not be so certain that a falling rate would soon start to rise again, or that a rising rate would soon start to fall. They might consequently buy as rates began to rise or sell as rates began to fall, and might then aggravate price fluctuations. The importance of a "normal" rate showed up clearly in the 1950's, when the Canadian dollar was allowed to fluctuate: the exchange rate stayed within a rather narrow range, helped by speculation. But the speculators may have been guided by a fixed norm—the old one-for-one parity between the two currencies. The behavior of the spot and forward rates supports this hypothesis. When the Canadian dollar exceeded its old parity with the U.S. dollar, it dropped to a discount on the forward market; speculators apparently thought the spot rate was "too high," basing their opinions on the old parity.[4]

This need for a "normal" rate implies that exchange-rate flexibility may work most efficiently when the underlying balance-of-payments disturbances do not call for large variations in the rate. If large changes are required and the rate drifts away from its familiar range, speculators may not know which way to turn and may begin to operate in a destabilizing manner.

There is one more objection to full flexibility: it could build an upward bias into world prices. Depreciations and devaluations raise the domestic prices of imported goods; this is how they work to discourage imports. In countries that import foodstuffs or industrial materials, however, an increase in import prices raises the cost of living and evokes a demand for higher wages. Higher wages, in turn, raise prices further—including export prices. In brief, an exchange-rate change can touch off a wage-price spiral, offsetting much of the competitive advantage conferred by the initial depreciation or devaluation. If, of course, the increase in wage rates is quite small compared to the de-

[4] Paul Wonnacott, *The Canadian Dollar, 1948-1962* (Toronto: University of Toronto Press, 1965), p. 188.

preciation, the depreciation will still serve to eliminate a payments deficit, and a country facing a deep-seated payments problem should accept depreciation. But what of a country whose foreign transactions display a cyclical pattern, showing a deficit during a boom and a surplus during a recession? If its exchange rate fluctuated freely, its currency would depreciate during a boom, adding to domestic inflationary pressures. It would, of course, appreciate during the next recession, but its wage rates might not come back down. With flexible exchange rates, then, the domestic business cycle would raise wages and prices in a step-wise fashion.

One could adduce another dozen arguments on each side of this issue— and as many intermediate positions. Some economists, for example, argue that fixed parities are needed, if only to provide speculators with the necessary "norm," but advocate wider margins for fluctuations on each side of parity. These wider margins, they contend, would raise the cost of speculating against a weak currency. If the pound could fall as low as $2.70 and rise as high as $2.90, speculators could lose 20¢ on the pound over a single swing, and 20¢ on $2.80 is a 7 per cent loss, much larger than the present 1.4 per cent.

But governments have not yet accepted the case for flexibility, nor for a wider band surrounding fixed parities. Indeed, official thinking has drifted the other way. The Canadian dollar was allowed to fluctuate for almost 12 years, then was pegged again in 1962. And most central banks oppose any change in the price of a key currency (the dollar, pound, franc, mark, or lira), fearing that a single change would touch off rumors of a second and third, as with the 1961 appreciation of the deutschemark. They apparently prefer to use their reserves in support of the existing exchange rates and to adjust their domestic policies whenever a major imbalance appears, requiring a lasting change in flows of trade or capital.

The New Gold-Exchange Standard

The central banks would seem to have sufficient reserves both for combating speculation in the foreign-exchange markets and for buying time in which to make gradual adjustments. At the end of 1965, central banks and governments held some $70 billion of gold and foreign currencies (Table 5-1), a sum nearly half as large as the dollar value of world exports, and many times larger than the largest annual reserve flow (the sum of all deficits) in recent years. Most of these reserves, moreover, were held at the center of the international monetary system. A full $41 billion belonged to eight governments—the United States, the United Kingdom, and six countries of the European Common Market. Furthermore, the center countries have substantial drawing rights on the International Monetary Fund,[5] and have

---

[5] So-called *gold-tranche* drawing rights are included in reserves, as shown in Table 5-2, for they correspond to the gold subscriptions governments made to obtain their quotas in the IMF, and may be drawn automatically when countries are in deficit. But drawing rights beyond the *gold tranche* are not included because they are not automatic.

established an impressive network of bilateral credit arrangements, giving them access to each other's currencies when they need to supplement their national reserves. Consequently, most authorities are satisfied with the present level of world reserves, though many are worried about their distribution, composition, and future expansion.

Table 5-1 INTERNATIONAL MONETARY RESERVES, 1955 AND 1965
(Billions of dollars; end of year)

Country or Area	1955	1965
United States	22.8	15.4
United Kingdom	2.4	3.0
Total, reserve centers	25.2	18.4
European Economic Community *	8.7	22.9
Canada and Japan	3.1	5.2
Other developed countries †	4.1	8.3
Total, all developed countries	41.1	54.8
Other European countries	2.5	4.2
Latin America	3.3	3.4
Other Asian and African countries	7.4	7.8
Total, less-developed countries	13.2	15.4
Total, all countries	54.3	70.2

* Belgium-Luxembourg, France, Germany, Italy and the Netherlands.
† Austria, Denmark, Norway, Sweden, Switzerland, Australia, New Zealand, and South Africa.

Source: International Monetary Fund, *International Financial Statistics* (various issues).

During the past decade or so, continental Europe has increased its reserves at a very rapid rate; indeed the EEC by itself added $14 billion to its holdings between 1955 and 1965. But Britain has stood still for more than a decade, and does not have enough reserves, given the importance of sterling as an international currency. Furthermore, the less-developed countries have gained very little, and lack the cash assets required to deal with their payments problems. It is sometimes said that the low-income countries would *spend* any increase in reserves because they need foreign exchange for development—that any redistribution of reserves would not last long because the low-income countries would soon run down their holdings to their original low levels. This is probably true, but does not dispel concern that those levels are too low and that, in consequence, the less-developed countries are forced into premature policy measures, including resort to import restrictions, whenever they lapse into deficit.

Concern about the composition of reserves has grown acutely in the past few years. Outside the United States, reserves are evenly divided between gold and currencies (see Table 5-2). The U.S. dollar is the leading reserve currency, accounting for a quarter of other countries' reserve assets. But the United States has actually supplied more than half of the increase in other

83

countries' reserves since 1955. It has furnished $6.0 billion of dollar assets and $7.7 billion of gold (the other $6.6 billion of gold coming from new production and Soviet sales). The $7.7 billion gold loss and $6.0 billion increase in U.S. debts are the consequence of deficits in the United States balance of payments.

Table 5-2 THE COMPOSITION OF INTERNATIONAL MONETARY RESERVES, 1955 AND 1965 (Billions of dollars; end of year)

Country and Asset	1955	1965
United States	22.8	15.4
Gold	21.8	14.1
Foreign exchange *	1.0	1.3
All other countries	31.5	54.8
Gold	13.6	27.9
Foreign exchange *	17.9	26.9
U.S. dollars	8.3	14.3
Sterling	7.6	6.7
IMF gold-tranche positions	0.9	4.8
Other †	1.1	1.1

* Includes *gold-tranche* drawing rights on the International Monetary Fund.

† Derived as a residual (the difference between total foreign-exchange assets reported by the holders and the foreign-exchange liabilities reported by the United States and United Kingdom; the 1965 figure may include some dollars held outside the United States and some official holdings of long-term dollar securities.

Source: International Monetary Fund, *International Financial Statistics* (various issues).

The United States is far from insolvency, despite this deterioration in its own reserve position. Table 5-3 shows that the total foreign assets of the United States greatly exceed its total liabilities, and that the excess of assets over liabilities has grown tremendously since 1950. But many observers are not impressed with this calculation; they look, instead, at the U.S. cash position, and this has weakened markedly. There has been a $7.6 billion decline in the official monetary assets of the United States and a $16.3 billion increase in its liabilities to foreign governments and central banks, making for a $23.9 billion decline in the net figure.[6]

A few years ago, no one would have talked of a run on the dollar, but such talk is heard frequently today. In fact, there was a short-lived run on the dollar late in 1960, when private investors and a handful of governments cashed in dollar assets to buy gold, and drove the free-market price of gold from $35 to $42 an ounce. More recently, some central banks, including the Bank of France, have run down their dollar holdings.

[6] Some people are also concerned about the $5.9 billion increase in U.S. short-term obligations to other foreigners, and do not take much comfort from the $9.2 billion increase in U.S. private short-term claims, for those include bank loans and commercial credits which the government could not mobilize easily in order to defend the dollar.

Table 5-3 THE INTERNATIONAL INVESTMENT POSITION
OF THE UNITED STATES, 1950 AND 1964
(Billions of dollars; end of year)

Item	1950	1964
Total Assets	**54.4**	**114.2**
Official monetary assets (gold and foreign exchange)	24.3	16.7
Private monetary assets (claims on foreigners)	1.5	10.7
Private direct investments abroad	11.8	44.3
Other private long-term investments abroad	5.7	20.4
Other government claims on foreigners	11.1	22.1
Total Liabilities	**17.6**	**56.8**
Monetary liabilities to foreign governments *	3.7	20.0
Monetary liabilities to other foreigners	5.9	11.8
Foreign private direct investments	3.4	8.4
Other foreign long-term investments	4.6	16.6
Excess of Assets over Liabilities:		
All assets less all liabilities	**36.8**	**57.4**
Official monetary assets less official monetary liabilities	**20.6**	**− 3.3**

* Figure for 1964 includes certain U.S. obligations that do not appear in the corresponding 1965 total of dollar reserves given in Table 5-2.

Source: United States Department of Commerce, Survey of Current Business (September, 1965); and Board of Governments of the Federal Reserve System, Banking and Monetary Statistics, Supplement 15 (March, 1962).

Doubts about the dollar, reflected in these recent trends, are premature. The United States still holds a third of the world's gold, and though the dollar holdings of foreign governments are larger than U.S. reserves, those dollars are widely held and most of them are firmly lodged. No single government could carry off a large part of the U.S. gold stock, and few would be inclined to try. Most governments and central banks have come to recognize that a major run on the dollar would be an attack upon the stability of the international monetary system itself, and such an attack would damage the trade and payments of the entire international community. Yet many experts have grave doubts about the long-run prospect. They fear that the present connection between the United States balance of payments and the U.S. balance sheet as an international banker may be unhealthy for the United States and for the international monetary system.

The assets and liabilities of an ordinary commercial bank move in the same direction. When its customers draw down their deposits, the bank's cash holdings and liabilities fall together. But the cash assets and liabilities of the United States, acting as an international bank, may move in opposite directions because its balance sheet is linked with its transactions as a producer, consumer, and investor—with its balance of payments. When the United States slips into deficit, it loses gold and, simultaneously, incurs additional deposit obligations to foreign governments. Its cash position tends to deteriorate at the very time when the outside world comes into possession of additional dollars. If, then, the United States runs a large or long deficit in its international transactions, its depositors may not want to hold more dollars—or those they already possess—and may then compound the payments problems of the United States by cashing in their dollars. Concerned that these difficulties may become more serious over the next several years, governments and academic economists have been seeking to alter the connection between the United States' balance of payments and the international monetary system— to forestall any sudden switch from dollars to gold and to furnish an increase in total reserves when such an increase is needed.

These two tasks are closely connected. To forestall a shift from dollars to gold, the United States must eliminate its payments deficit, for this would bolster confidence in the dollar as a reserve currency. But when it has done so, the growth of total reserves will slow down. U.S. deficits have been the chief source of reserves for other countries, and new gold production plus Soviet gold sales may not furnish sufficient additional reserves to meet future needs. It has been suggested that governments might then increase the price of gold, as this would raise the dollar value of existing gold stocks and stimulate new gold production. But an increase in the price of gold might aggravate the problem of stability, by damaging confidence in the dollar.

The Role of the International Monetary Fund

Most proposals for reform of the international monetary system look to a strengthening or reconstruction of the International Monetary Fund. As presently constituted, the IMF cannot create reserves in significant amounts, but does make them "go around" more efficiently. It is a pool of currencies and gold furnished by its 103 member governments. When a country joins the IMF, it is assigned a *quota* which governs the size of its cash subscription, its voting power, and its drawing rights. The United States has the largest quota ($5,160 million), Lebanon the smallest ($6.75 million). A member country pays a quarter of its quota in gold and the balance in its own currency. Thus, the United States has paid in $1,290 million of gold and $3,870 million of special U.S. government securities.

When a country encounters a payments deficit and does not have sufficient reserves to cope with the problem, it can buy foreign currencies from the IMF in exchange for its own currency, but it must repurchase its own currency within five years. A member of the IMF is always entitled to buy foreign currencies equal in value to a quarter of its quota (the equivalent of its initial gold subscription, or *gold tranche*). To make a larger purchase, it must satisfy the Fund that it is trying to solve its payments problem, as by controlling domestic inflation. Thus, the Fund is able to exert a unique influence on national policies. In the words of a former Fund official:

    ... when a country is clearly in such an unbalanced position that radical measures are required to restore equilibrium, private banks may properly be deterred by the risks involved in granting it further credit facilities. In such situations, it is only if a comprehensive program is adopted and put into effect that the risks will be reduced; and private institutions are not in a position to negotiate such programs. Experience has shown that the Governments in the various countries are more willing to discuss and work out stabilization programs with officials of the Fund than with representatives of other countries or of private credit institutions.

The IMF has proved its usefulness. In 19 years, it supplied 16 different currencies to 58 countries in amounts totaling $11.5 billion. Britain has been the largest single beneficiary of IMF assistance, as Britain's own reserves are very small and foreign observers have forecast a devaluation of the pound whenever Britain has run into deficit. The less-developed countries have also made extensive use of IMF resources. They, too, have small reserves and chronic payments problems. Their imports have risen rapidly because of their efforts to stimulate development. And most of them earn their way in world trade by exporting raw materials such as coffee, tin, and copper—products that are subject to wide price fluctuations.

Because of its great success and the respect it enjoys, many proponents of reform have urged an expansion of the IMF to improve the world's monetary system.

First, they advocate a periodic revision in IMF quotas and a liberalization of the rules that regulate drawing rights. A continuous growth in quotas, they maintain, could substitute for a straightforward increase in national reserves. Admittedly, governments would have to put more gold into the IMF to obtain larger quotas. But they would obtain a $4 increase in quotas (and a larger increase in drawing rights) for every dollar's worth of gold paid in.

Second, they advocate special arrangements to protect the key currencies against speculation and to forestall shifts in reserve composition. Although total IMF assets exceed $20 billion, *usable* assets are much smaller. At the end of 1965, IMF holdings of gold and major currencies looked like this:

Gold	$ 2.7 billion
United States dollars	3.5 "
Sterling	3.9 "
EEC currencies	0.5 "
Other key currencies	0.6 "
Total	$11.2 "

And the Fund cannot use all these assets at the same time. If the U.S. dollar were in trouble, the Fund could not use dollars to help out; it would have to use gold and other convertible currencies and might not have enough to combat a wave of speculation against a key currency.

This two-part proposal has already found favor in official circles and the Fund has been moving far along these lines. In 1959 and 1965, Fund quotas were enlarged considerably. In 1962, 10 key countries, including the United States, agreed on procedures for lending to the IMF should it need additional assets to finance a major drawing. This agreement is not automatic, nor is it sufficiently flexible; each government retains full freedom of action and can refuse to lend anything at all. But most of them would probably honor their pledges if the IMF needed extra cash.

The IMF has also shown how it can help to combat speculation against a key currency. It did so directly during the Suez crisis of 1956, when it supplied $561 million to Great Britain and frightened off the speculators. It did so indirectly in 1961 and 1964, when it *refinanced* a series of special bilateral credit arrangements between Britain and other countries. On both occasions, Britain suffered large outflows of short-term capital and came near to exhausting its reserves. Other central banks came to her aid by buying pounds in the foreign-exchange market and lending their own currencies to the British government. Thereafter, Britain drew foreign currencies from the IMF ($1.5 billion in 1961 and a full $2.4 billion in 1964-1965), using some of this money to repay the central banks. In effect, the Fund consolidated Britain's bilateral indebtedness. In 1964-1965, moreover, the IMF invoked its special agreement with the so-called Group of Ten, borrowing $930 million in eight currencies to finance Britain's drawing.

But many proponents of reform, while welcoming a stronger IMF, are still dissatisfied. They would like to sever any connection between the U.S. balance of payments and the creation of reserves, because American deficits could still undermine the monetary system and because the United States cannot change its own exchange rate without breaking the link between gold and the dollar, the two most important reserve assets. Finally, the critics say, an increase in IMF quotas may not be a satisfactory substitute for larger reserves because drawings on the Fund must be repaid.

The leading advocate of thorough reform is Professor Robert Triffin of Yale. He has suggested that the International Monetary Fund be transformed into a central bankers' bank—that central banks deposit a percentage of their gross reserves with the IMF, and that these deposits be denominated in a new international unit of account.[7]

This arrangement, Triffin says, would have two advantages. First, deposits at the IMF would carry a gold guarantee. If there were an increase in the dollar price of gold (a devaluation of the dollar), the value of an IMF deposit would not be affected, whereas a dollar deposit would buy less gold thereafter. Governments would have little cause to change the composition of their reserves. Second, the IMF could enlarge total reserves in much the same way that a national central bank enlarges the reserves of the commercial banks. It could create a new type of money. Instead of selling foreign currency

[7] Triffin suggests that they be required to deposit 20 per cent of their reserves, but believes that most governments would voluntarily keep a larger fraction on deposit with the IMF, as these deposits would earn interest and be guaranteed against exchange-rate changes. Triffin's plan, incidentally, has distinguished antecedents, including a proposal by Lord Keynes, offered as an alternative to the United States' plan for the IMF when the Fund was set up in 1944.

to a country needing more reserves, the Fund would make straightforward loans, creating new deposits to the credit of the borrower. The borrower could then draw on its deposit to settle deficits with other governments—or could use its balance to buy foreign currencies for use in the foreign-exchange markets. Finally, the IMF would be authorized to buy national securities in the open market, much in the manner of a central bank conducting open-market operations, so as to create more IMF money and thereby enlarge world reserves.

Triffin's plan would limit lending by the IMF, to guarantee against an excessive expansion of world reserves. It could be no larger than required to augment reserves by 3 or 4 per cent a year. His plan would also allow a central bank to convert its "excess" IMF deposits into gold or currency—to dispose of deposits it was not obliged to hold under the prevailing reserve ratio. Thus, no country would have to accept indefinite amounts of IMF deposit money.

Other plans have been devised to repair apparent defects in Triffin's proposal. Still others would connect the creation of new reserves to the international financing of economic development. Under these plans, the IMF would buy bonds from intergovernmental agencies like the International Bank for Reconstruction and Development, supplying these agencies with IMF deposits which could then be lent to the less-developed countries.

But all these plans have met with frowns from the central bankers and finance ministers. There is an understandable resistance to radical reform—which goes deeper than doubts about technicalities. A prominent American spokesman has summarized official views:

> The money created by a super-bank would be the most high-powered ever generated by a man-made institution, yet it would have no supporting super-government to make good on its debts or claims. Even with all the underlying resources of the richest nation on earth, the performance of the United States in providing additional reserves has been at times rather conspicuously called into question. And in our case, the world has the basic assurance that our performance will continue broadly to meet the tests of economic requirements because otherwise pressures can be exerted upon us through our own balance of payments. There will be no comparable assurance, and no comparable underlying strength in the new body.[8]

The governments, however, have not been wholly hostile to proposals for reform. In carefully negotiated language, the Group of Ten conceded that existing arrangements may not be adequate, and authorized the start of serious official planning to revamp the gold-exchange standard:

> Looking further into the future, since there is a possibility that the supply of gold and foreign-exchange reserves may prove to be inadequate

---

[8] Robert V. Roosa, "Assuring the Free World's Liquidity," *Business Review Supplement,* Federal Reserve Bank of Philadelphia (September, 1962), p. 8.

for the over-all reserve needs of the world economy, the Ministers . . . , without prejudging any aspect of this question, have approved the arrangements made by their Deputies for a study group to examine various proposals regarding the creation of reserve assets either through the IMF or otherwise.[9]

Their Deputies, in turn, have come close to agreement on plans to create a new "collective reserve unit" (CRU) outside the IMF. The CRU would be issued to a limited group of industrial countries who would deposit their own currencies to "back" the new unit. The CRU would be distributed and used according to formulae reflecting the participants' gold holdings or reserves, so that the supply of new reserve assets would not be connected to surpluses and deficits, as under Triffin's plan for IMF lending. Furthermore, the CRU would not replace existing reserve assets and would not be convertible into gold or dollars. They would merely supplement existing reserves.

The original plans to create this new asset would have limited its distribution to the industrial countries, and the less-developed countries expressed concern that they would be denied an increase in their reserves. A modified proposal, still under study, would transfer a fixed fraction of the new units to the International Monetary Fund, allowing the IMF to offer extra drawing rights to the less-developed countries without asking those countries to pay in more gold.

THE UNITED STATES
PAYMENTS PROBLEM

All of the proposals for creating new reserves—radical and modest, private and official—have one thing in common: they require an end to the large deficit in the United States' balance of payments. No amount of financing, no special arrangements, can sustain international confidence in the U.S. dollar if our gold holdings continue to shrink and our liabilities continue to grow. Hence, elimination of the payments deficit has become a major policy target.

The United States has run payments deficits since the early 1950's. In the late 1950's, however, its deficits grew very large, and averaged about $2 billion yearly from 1958 through 1965. Part of this increase in the deficit can be blamed on the inflation of the 1950's. Table 5-4 shows that U.S. export prices rose rather rapidly from 1955 through 1960. The over-all (consumer) price index did not behave badly when compared to the price indexes of other countries, but a sharp advance in steel prices raised many export prices. The United States did not lose too much ground in world markets, but neither did it gain sufficiently to cover its growing import bill, its military spending, or the surge in private foreign investment.

[9] *Ministerial Statement of the Group of Ten*, August 1964, ¶5. The Group of Ten includes the United States, Belgium, Canada, France, Germany, Italy, Japan, the Netherlands, Sweden, and the United Kingdom.

Table 5-4 PERCENTAGE INCREASE IN PRICES, MAJOR INDUSTRIAL COUNTRIES, 1955 TO 1960 AND 1960 TO 1965

Country	Consumer Prices *		Export Prices *	
	1955-1960	1960-1965	1955-1960	1960-1965
United States	+10	+ 7	+ 7	+ 5
Belgium	+10	+11	0	0
Canada	+10	+ 9	+ 6	— 3
France	+32	+20	— 1	+ 5
Germany	+ 8	+16	+ 5	+ 8
Italy	+10	+27	— 8	— 2
Japan	+10	+35	— 4	— 5
Netherlands	+13	+22	0	+10
Sweden	+19	+19	0	+ 5
Switzerland	+ 6	+17	0	+15
United Kingdom	+11	+20	+ 9	+ 8

* Corrected for changes in exchange rates relative to the dollar.

Source: International Monetary Fund, International Financial Statistics (various issues).

In the early 1960's, U.S. prices rose somewhat less rapidly than those of other countries, and the U.S. trade balance improved dramatically; from 1960 through 1964, average annual merchandise exports were $5.3 billion larger than merchandise imports (see Table 5-5). Furthermore, our earnings on foreign investments were $3.3 billion larger than foreign earnings in the United States. Yet the payments deficit did not subside, for there was a further increase in military spending, foreign aid, and private investment. In the five-year period 1960-1964, net outlays on foreign aid (grants and loans) and military spending averaged $5.5 billion, and U.S. private investment (including private cash flows) accounted for $4.6 billion more. In 1965, moreover, a rapid expansion of the domestic economy led to larger imports, shrinking the trade balance to $4.8 billion, and private investment continued to run at a high level, despite the introduction of "voluntary" capital controls.

The United States has taken many measures to reduce the deficit. In the 1950's, it "tied" most of its foreign aid to the purchase of American goods and services and cut down on overseas spending by its armed forces, compelling the Defense Department to "buy American" whenever possible. In effect, it imposed a covert tariff on government spending abroad, forcing government agencies (and the taxpayer) to spend more for goods and services. Then, in 1963, the United States imposed a tax on purchases of foreign securities (except those of Canada and the less-developed countries), and in 1965, applied this same tax to long-term foreign loans by U.S. banks. It also asked the banks to hold down their foreign loans, and made a similar appeal to companies with foreign branches or affiliates, asking that they postpone or pare their new capital commitments and that they borrow abroad for projects that cannot be postponed. Finally, in 1965 and 1966, the Federal Reserve

Table 5-5 THE U.S. BALANCE OF PAYMENTS,
1960-1964 AND 1965 (Billions of dollars)

Item	Average 1960-1964	1965
Exports of goods and services	31.1	39.0
Merchandise exports	21.5	26.3
Transport, travel, and other services	4.6	6.0
Military receipts	0.6	0.8
Income on U.S. investments abroad	4.4	5.9
Imports of goods and services	−25.2	−32.0
Merchandise imports	−16.2	−21.5
Transport, travel, and other services	− 4.9	− 6.0
Military expenditures	− 3.0	− 2.9
Income on foreign investments in U.S.	− 1.1	− 1.6
Unilateral transfers (net)	− 2.6	− 2.8
Government grants	− 1.8	− 1.8
Other transfers	− 0.8	− 1.0
Balance on current account	3.3	4.2
Capital account [net outflow (−)]	− 4.4	− 5.5
U.S. government credits and claims	− 1.3	− 1.6
U.S. private direct investment abroad	− 1.9	− 3.4
Other U.S. private lending and investment abroad	− 1.7	− 0.6
Foreign investment and lending in U.S.	0.5	0.1
Errors and omissions (net)	− 0.9	− 0.4
Balance on current and capital accounts	− 2.0	− 1.7
Cash account		
Private holdings and claims	− 0.2	0.4
U.S. claims on foreigners [increase (−)]	− 1.0	0.3
Foreign claims on U.S. [increase (+)]	0.8	0.1
Official holdings and claims [net deficit]	− 2.2	1.3
U.S. reserve assets [increase (−)]	1.0	1.2
Foreign official dollar holdings [increase (+)]	1.2	0.1

Source: United States Department of Commerce, *Survey of Current Business* (June, 1966). Private holdings and claims in the cash account are those reported by U.S. banks; all other short-term credits and claims appear in the capital account. Foreign official dollar holdings are those used to compute the official settlements measure of the deficit; all other official claims appear as foreign investment in the U.S.

System began to pursue a more restrictive monetary policy, partly to curb domestic inflation but also to discourage capital outflows and to attract foreign funds.

What more can be done to end the payments deficit? Some people have urged that the United States make further cuts in foreign aid, or slash its military spending abroad by pulling some of its troops out of Western Europe. At first glance, after all, these seem to be the troublemakers. But the problem is not quite so simple. If the United States reduced its foreign aid, exports would fall, too, eroding the current-account surplus. Of the $4.3 billion in new grants and loans furnished in 1965, fully $3.6 billion were spent in the United States. What is more important, foreign aid and military spending are vital parts of larger American policies shaped to foster the security and prosperity of friendly countries. From the standpoint of the balance of payments, they must be taken as given, and other transactions must be adjusted in order to make room for them.

But this is not easy, either. Any other country confronting such a problem could resort to devaluation—which would enlarge its exports, reduce its imports, and make room for capital or government transactions—but the United States is not free to do so. A devaluation of the dollar would undoubtedly improve our balance of payments, but it would rupture the link between gold and the dollar, damaging the monetary system. In addition, a devaluation of the dollar is apt to provoke retaliation, by improving our competitive position, it would damage the foreign trade of other countries, including some countries that do not have surpluses. Those countries, including Canada, Japan, and the United Kingdom, would probably be forced to devalue alongside us, and the process might well spread, as in the 1930's, for its impact would come to be concentrated on a smaller and smaller cluster of countries that had not yet changed their exchange rates. In the end, there might be little change in the system of exchange rates, and very little benefit to the United States.

There has, of course, been gradual improvement in the United States' balance of payments. (Compare the five-year averages for 1960-1964 with the separate figures for 1965 given in Table 5-5.) The more rapid increase of European prices and the several growth effects discussed in Chapter 4 have been taking hold. Yet the payments problem may not vanish soon, and additional remedies may be required. These may well include *ad hoc* measures that border on exchange control, covert trade barriers like the tying of foreign aid, and the classic remedies that governments are loath to take: restrictive monetary and fiscal policies to slow down the domestic economy.

SUMMARY

Long before the end of the Second World War, governments began to plan the reconstruction of the international monetary system. Determined to avoid another round of competitive exchange-rate changes like the one that followed the First World War, they decided to establish new exchange rates at the very start of the post-war period and to foster orderly changes thereafter. In the Bretton Woods agreement of 1944 establishing the International Monetary Fund, they agreed to forego devaluations, save on occasions of "fundamental disequilibrium."

93

One can make a strong case against the present system. By pegging the exchange rates, it fixes the one set of prices that could be changed with sufficient ease and speed to maintain payments equilibrium. And by compromising between a perfect fixity and full flexibility, it invites destabilizing capital movements that add to payments deficits. Finally, one can argue that a free market would choose the "right" exchange rate more accurately than a finance minister or central banker.

Yet there are telling objections to full flexibility too, and some of the defects of the present system could be removed if the gold-exchange standard were strengthened or reformed—if exchange rates could vary more widely around their fixed parities and if the supply of reserves could be disconnected from the American balance of payments.

You have met several plans fashioned to attain these aims—plans to increase quotas in the IMF and lend the Fund additional cash; plans to transform the IMF into an international central bank that could create reserves on its own initiative; and plans to create a "collective reserve unit" that would be held and used along with gold and dollars.

Finally, you have glanced at the U.S. payments problem and examined the constraints on American policy that make it so difficult for the United States to end its payments deficit. All of the issues and policy conflicts described in Chapter 4 find ample expression in the American experience—and all of the temptations to restrict foreign trade and payments are manifest in recent American policy.

CHAPTER SIX

THE CENTER AND PERIPHERY

A country's economic history has a tremendous effect on its comparative advantage; indeed, its stocks of capital and skill may influence its foreign trade more than its store of raw materials, climate, or terrain do. These stocks are the legacies of economic history—of investments made in years gone by. And these investments, in their turn, reflect still earlier trade patterns and market opportunities. The evolution of the international economy has been a cumulative process. Export opportunities, affecting the volume and pattern of investment, have shaped each country's stock of capital equipment. Those stocks of equipment, with the skills that accompany them, gave rise to new production possibilities, creating new trade patterns.

Foreign trade has been especially significant for the economic development of new countries, including the United States. Their resource endowments—their stocks of capital and skill—were shaped by their contact with the older countries of the international economy. As John Henry Williams of Harvard has put it:

> ... the development of international trade has been a process in which the countries outside the centre have owed the development of their trade, and indeed their very existence, to the movement, not merely of goods but of capital, labour, and entrepreneurship from the centre; and the centre countries have in turn owed their further development primarily to this movement.

95

Western Europe created the modern world and was in turn remade by it. Any theory of international trade that does not approach the subject-matter in this way must have very serious limitations as a guide to policy.[1]

And the late Ragnar Nurkse of Columbia dwelt on this same theme:

> ... The industrial revolution happened to originate on a small island with a limited range of natural resources, at a time when synthetic materials were yet unknown. In these circumstances economic expansion was transmitted to less-developed areas by a steep and steady increase in Britain's demand for primary commodities which those areas were well suited to produce. Local factors of production overseas, whose growth may in part have been induced by trade, were thus largely absorbed by the expansion of profitable primary production for export. On top of this, the center's increasing demand for raw materials and foodstuffs created incentives for capital and labor to move from the center to the outlying areas, accelerating the process of growth-transmission from the former to the latter.[2]

Some economists hold to the hope that trade can still serve as an "engine of growth" to quicken the development of Africa, Asia, and Latin America, and that private capital will venture out from the center of the world economy—from the United States and Europe—to find new raw materials and create new industries. But others are not as optimistic. They believe that the center must make special efforts to aid economic development. Otherwise, powerful disintegrative tendencies will widen the great gulf between rich and poor.

First, they point out that the new countries of the nineteenth century were quite different from today's less-developed countries. The United States, Canada, and Australia lay in temperate zones and had vast quantities of land with very little labor. They could supply the grain and cotton Europe required. Furthermore, they were peopled by immigrants with European institutions and values. Most of today's less-developed countries, by contrast, lie in the tropics and are densely populated. What may be more important, they are not mere islands of European civilization, but have institutions and values of their own.

Second, trade patterns have changed since the nineteenth century. The center countries' need for raw materials is not growing the way it did in the nineteenth century. Production at the center tends to be resource-saving rather than resource-using; the raw-materials content of national output is a smaller fraction of the whole than a century ago; value added by processing is very much larger. Furthermore, the development of synthetic materials has greatly reduced the demand for some raw materials, notably cotton and wool.

[1] John H. Williams, *Trade, Not Aid: A Program for World Stability*. The Stamp Memorial Lecture, 1952 (Cambridge: Harvard University Press, 1953), p. 10.

[2] Ragnar Nurkse, "Patterns of Trade and Development," reprinted in *Equilibrium and Growth in the World Economy* (Cambridge: Harvard University Press, 1961), p. 285.

Third, the less-developed countries do not welcome private foreign capital because it has colonial overtones. Nor are they willing forever to remain suppliers of raw materials. They fear the continued instability of raw-materials prices and foresee a downward trend. They are inclined to draw back from dependence on world markets. Above all, they identify development with industrialization, and seek to build modern industrial facilities to symbolize their independence and assert their maturity. How closely they follow the ancient advice of Alexander Hamilton's *Report on Manufactures:*

> ... the foreign demand for the products of agricultural countries, is in a great degree, rather casual and occasional, than certain or constant ... there are natural causes tending to render the external demand for the surplus of agricultural nations a precarious reliance. . . .
>
> Considering how fast and how much the progress of new settlements in the United States must increase the surplus produce of the soil ... there appear strong reasons to regard the foreign demand for that surplus as too uncertain a reliance, and to desire a substitute for it, in an extensive domestic market.
>
> To secure such a market, there is no other expedient, than to promote manufacturing establishments.

The Network of World Trade

Recent trends in world trade support this pessimistic view. In 1964, world exports totaled $149 billion; they were about one-fifth as large as the gross national product of the United States. But fully half of world exports stayed inside the center of the world economy. The industrial countries imported only $33 billion worth of goods from the periphery, a mere 19 per cent of world imports and a small fraction of the total imports of the industrial countries themselves.[3] Yet this thin trade-flow between center and periphery is the one that must transmit the impulse to growth. Furthermore, this vital flow has grown more slowly than trade within the industrial center. The dollar value of trade within the center increased by 166 per cent between 1953 and 1964, while the dollar value of imports from outside grew by a mere 37 per cent.

In one important case, center-country imports have grown quite rapidly, and certain less-developed countries have prospered accordingly. The demand for petroleum has pumped foreign capital into the Middle East, North Africa, and Venezuela, which have used their oil revenues to finance development. The oil-rich countries pay large profits to the foreign oil companies, but can still live far beyond their ordinary means. The huge payments surplus of the oil sector finances a gaping payments deficit for the rest of the economy, paying for imported capital equipment and consumer goods.

[3] The "industrial/non-industrial" classification used in Table 6-1 does not exactly match the "developed/less-developed" classification. Japan is an industrial country, but by the test of income per capita is much less developed than Australia or New Zealand, which are classified here as non-industrial countries. But there is at least a rough correspondence between the two sets of categories.

Table 6-1   TRADE BETWEEN INDUSTRIAL
AND NON-INDUSTRIAL COUNTRIES IN 1964

Trade Flow	Value in Billions of Dollars	Percentage of World Trade *	Percentage Change Since 1953
1. World exports (= world imports) *	148.7	100	+112
2. Exports of industrial countries †	109.3	73	+139
2a. To industrial countries	76.3	51	+166
2b. To non-industrial countries	33.0	22	+ 93
3. Exports of non-industrial countries	39.4	27	+ 61
3a. To industrial countries	27.8	19	+ 37
3b. To non-industrial countries	11.6	8	+ 68
4. Imports of industrial countries (2a + 3a)	104.1	70	+125
5. Imports of non-industrial countries (2b + 3b)	44.6	30	+ 86

* Excludes Soviet-bloc trade.
† North America, Western Europe, and Japan.

Source: General Agreement on Tariffs and Trade, *International Trade*, 1964.

But the petroleum producers face trouble, too. With the discovery of oil in North Africa and increased Soviet petroleum sales to non-communist countries, oil prices have weakened. The older producers have had to make room for new rivals, just as Brazil and Colombia have had to give way before the new coffee-growing countries of West Africa.

FIG. 6-1   The export and import prices of the less-developed countries. Following the sharp rise during the Korean War (1950-1951), the export prices of the less-developed countries started to decline, whereas their import prices stayed rather steady. Export prices rose in 1963-1964, but seem to be slipping again. (Source: United Nations indexes in International Monetary Fund, *International Financial Statistics*, various issues.)

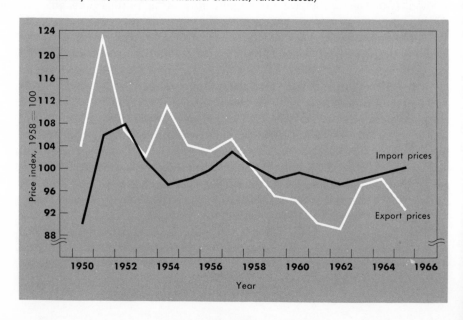

The Prices of Primary Products

The recent weakening of oil prices is part of a larger picture, for the prices of many primary products have been declining, with foodstuffs like cacao, tea, and coffee leading the way. Hence, average prices earned by the less-developed countries have been falling, compared to average prices paid (see Fig. 6-1). In some cases, moreover, the price decline has been quite sharp. As coffee accounts for some 60 per cent of Colombia's exports, the decline in coffee prices depressed Colombia's export price index by a full 22 per cent between 1955 and 1965 (see Fig. 6-2). The decline in cacao prices had a similar effect on Ghana's price index, which dropped by 36 per cent during that same period.

This downward trend has not been uniform. The prices of nonferrous metals have been rising steeply, so that countries like Bolivia, which exports tin, have enjoyed a remarkable increase in their export prices. But the number and severity of falling prices has caused deep concern, and is only half the problem that faces the less-developed countries; they must also cope with short-term fluctuations that can be very violent. The years 1955-1965 saw comparative stability in the world economy—yet there were huge swings in

FIG. 6-2 The change in export prices, 1955-1965, selected less-developed countries. The decline in the prices of key raw materials has been reflected in the average export prices of the less-developed countries that export one or two of those raw materials. (Source: International Monetary Fund, *International Financial Statistics*, various issues.)

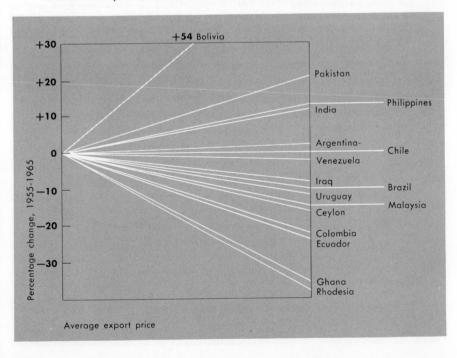

the prices of raw materials, with eight major products showing a *year-to-year* price decline greater than 20 per cent:[4]

Cacao	—27 per cent (1955-56)
Coconut oil	—26 per cent (1960-61)
Coffee	—21 per cent (1958-59)
Copper	—33 per cent (1956-57)
Copra	—29 per cent (1960-61)
Jute	—29 per cent (1961-62)
Rubber	—27 per cent (1960-61)
Wool	—29 per cent (1957-58)

This short-term instability is nothing new; it was in fact much more pronounced before the Second World War. But contemporary governments are much less tolerant of price fluctuations. The less-developed countries are committed to promoting economic stability, just like the countries of North America and Western Europe, although they do not always possess the policy instruments required to offset a serious disturbance such as a major price change. Furthermore, the instability of export prices is often mirrored in total export earnings. In fact, total receipts can change more than prices; when demand declines, price and quantity fall together, and price *times* quantity falls more than either one alone. Thus, the less-developed countries frequently confront sudden shortages of foreign currency and are then obliged to cut back their imports. Some of them have had to curb industrial investment, slowing down their planned development.

The Flow of Private Capital

In the nineteenth century there were two large flows of cash from center to periphery. Europe's demand for food and raw materials gave rise to the first; her lending gave rise to the second. Both flows reflected the center countries' need for raw materials; European capital went to the periphery to expand the supply of primary products. Some of it was invested directly in mining, plantation agriculture, and ranching, but most of it went into transportation and public utilities, helping to move goods rather than produce them. Thus, fully half the cash that built the American railroads in 1860-1880 came from abroad, mainly from Britain. Between 1860 and 1890, some $2.5 billion of foreign capital came to the United States, helping to finance imports of producers' goods, including railroad rolling-stock.

The less-developed countries of the twentieth century also need foreign funds to finance development. Foreign capital is a claim on foreign resources, and a country able to exercise such a claim can invest more than it saves. It can carry on more capital formation than would be possible if it were left to its own devices. As a matter of fact, the less-developed countries make more deliberate and systematic use of foreign capital than their predecessors in the

[4] International Monetary Fund, *International Financial Statistics,* various issues.

nineteenth century did. The American companies that borrowed abroad by selling securities in London were not trying consciously to supplement American resources. They did so because it was cheaper and easier to issue securities in London than in New York; the London bond market was better developed and the London dealers were expert in handling new issues. Today, by contrast, governments set out deliberately to supplement domestic savings by foreign borrowing. India's Third Five-Year Plan, covering 1961-1965, called for more than $20 billion of new investments—public and private, domestic and foreign. To reach this total, India required some $6 billion of foreign capital. Hence, the International Bank for Reconstruction and Development (IBRD) organized a *consortium* of capital-exporting countries, which pledged $5.5 billion in grants and public loans for the Five-Year Plan:

Canada	$ 173 million
France	120 "
Germany	645 "
Italy	170 "
Japan	290 "
United Kingdom	518 "
United States	2,285 "
Other countries	86 "
IBRD and affiliates	1,185 "
Total	$5,472 "

Some economists believe that the less-developed countries should be able to attract more private capital. They criticize India and other countries for relying so heavily on official funds. The United States, they say, managed to attract private investors—to borrow enormous sums in London and other European centers—so why can't India, Egypt, or Brazil? And why can't they attract direct investments from the United States and countries in Western Europe?

Unfortunately there are several flaws in the analogy between the less-developed countries of the nineteenth century and those of the twentieth. To begin with, most nineteenth-century capital transfers were portfolio investments (bond issues) rather than direct investments (the building of factories and other facilities by foreign companies). If, then, the less-developed countries were to follow the American example, they would borrow foreign money by issuing bonds. But the European and American markets for foreign securities were badly battered in the 1930's. There were large foreign bond flotations in the 1920's, but with the financial collapse that followed, this source of capital dried up. Many borrowers suspended interest payments and some of them defaulted on the principal. The New York market for foreign bonds has begun to revive; Canada, Japan, and European borrowers have floated large issues. Yet investors are still very chary of the less-developed countries which still have chronic payments problems and maintain exchange control. Furthermore, many of the less-developed countries have already borrowed hugely from foreign governments, the IBRD, and U.S. commercial banks, and

101

have thereby incurred heavy debt-service burdens, impairing foreign confidence in their credit-worthiness. Their long-term debts tripled between 1956 and 1964, and their annual payments of interest and principal mounted from 4 per cent of their export earnings to a full 12 per cent.[5]

Even in the nineteenth century, moreover, little foreign capital went into manufacturing—yet that is where the less-developed countries want it channeled now. Like many European countries, they have placed their public utilities and transportation systems under state ownership or close regulation.

Finally, the slow growth of demand for raw materials has deterred American companies from expanding their interests in mining and agriculture in the less-developed countries. For that matter, many of those countries are not anxious to attract foreign capital into extractive industries; they equate extraction with exploitation, and want to reduce their dependence on exports of raw materials.

Despite these fears and barriers, however, there has been a great deal of foreign investment in the periphery—more than one would forecast knowing all the circumstances. In each of the past several years, some $2 billion of new private capital has been forthcoming, half of it American (see Table 6-2).

Table 6-2   TOTAL FLOW OF CAPITAL TO THE LESS-DEVELOPED COUNTRIES AND TO INTERNATIONAL ORGANIZATIONS FINANCING DEVELOPMENT, 1964 (Millions of dollars)

Type of Capital and Source	Amount
Public Capital	$5,698
United States	3,206
Other countries	2,492
Government grants	2,553
Agricultural commodities	1,036
Long-term loans *	1,682
Contributions to international organizations	427
Private Capital	2,156
United States	1,201
Other countries	955
Direct investments †	1,547
Portfolio and other * ‡	609
Grand Total	7,854

    * Net of repayments.
    † Including reinvested earnings.
    ‡ Including private purchases of IBRD bonds.

Source: United Nations, *International Flow of Long-term Capital and Official Donations, 1961-1965*, New York, 1966, pp. 6-10.

The flow of capital has not been growing, as some have hoped it would, but neither has it shrunk, as pessimists forecast.

[5] Based on data for 37 less-developed countries; see International Monetary Fund, *Annual Report, 1965*, pp. 24-26.

POLICY AT THE CENTER

In 1964, the United Nations sponsored its first Conference on Trade and Development (UNCTAD). There, the less-developed countries set forth their goals, problems, and proposals with a clarity and force that drove the developed countries on to the defensive. The Final Act of UNCTAD issued a challenge that cannot be ignored: [6]

> Economic development and social progress should be the common concern of the whole international community. . . . Accordingly, all countries pledge themselves to pursue internal and external economic policies designed to accelerate economic growth throughout the world, and in particular to help promote, in developing countries, a rate of growth consistent with the need to bring about a substantial and steady increase in average income. . . .

If, of course, the center countries can manage their own economies, fostering steady growth, they will have discharged their chief obligation to the less-developed countries. If the center prospers, the periphery can prosper; if the center stagnates, the periphery will stagnate. If, further, the industrial center grows steadily, its governments will be free to deal with the problems of development; but if its economies stagnate or are plagued by instability, its governments are apt to be preoccupied with problems near to home and may neglect their obligations in the outside world.

To meet this challenge fully, however, the developed countries have also to take special account of the periphery when shaping their own economic policies. The commercial policies of the center countries can exert a decisive influence on the economic development of the periphery. Turned one way, they can draw the less-developed countries into the world economy to capture the full gains from trade; turned the other, they can force those countries to pull back from foreign trade and cultivate a wasteful self-sufficiency. The financial policies of the center countries are equally important. By encouraging private foreign investment and supplying more official funds, the center can help the periphery to speed up capital formation, and so to grow more rapidly. Failing to do so, it may doom the less-developed countries to continued poverty, because population growth threatens to outstrip capital formation in many less-developed countries.

Commercial Policy

Some of the commercial problems of the less-developed countries should not be blamed on center-country policies—nor can they be remedied by

[6] United Nations, *Trade and Development, Final Act and Report*, New York, 1964, p. 10.

changes in those policies. (To take one example, the advent of synthetic textile fibers such as rayon and dacron has held down the demand for cotton and wool, while the spread of cotton cultivation has enlarged the supply of natural fibers. These changes in demand and supply have depressed world prices and have done particular damage to the older producers.) But center-country policies have sometimes compounded the underlying problems of the low-income countries that export raw materials. For instance, the United States has limited its imports of lead and zinc in order to protect American miners, and this has injured Mexico and other producers. Injuries to exporters in low-income countries have also resulted from the United States' and Western Europe's quotas on their sugar imports (to protect domestic beet-sugar industries), and Europe's use of very high taxes on several other tropical products, including coffee, tea, and bananas. Although the duties on these last three items are not protective (Europe does not grow such tropical foods), they still do damage to the less-developed countries by raising the prices paid by consumers, and thereby reducing Europe's consumption. Furthermore, the European Common Market gives preferential treatment to its former colonies in Africa, discriminating against imports from Asia and Latin America.

The center countries' price-support policies do similar damage: the United States imposes import quotas on wheat, rye, cotton, and other major staples in order to defend its domestic support prices against import competition; the European Common Market will apply variable import duties to that same end. Finally, the United States sells its farm surpluses to the less-developed countries on terms that may hurt competing producers and may even injure the recipient countries. Under the Food for Peace program, the U.S. government sells surplus wheat and other farm products for foreign currencies rather than dollars, allowing the less-developed countries to increase their food imports without using up their precious export earnings. The program has been praised for warding off famine in countries with food deficits (especially India), but has sometimes been accused of displacing the food exports of other low-income countries and of causing the recipient countries to rely on U.S. food, rather than developing their own food production. This last charge, if true, is a grave indictment, for U.S. food surpluses are coming to an end with the growth of domestic consumption and ordinary exports, and the less-developed countries must begin to build up their own food supplies.

Over the long run, however, the center countries' policies toward manufactured imports may have the strongest impact on the periphery. If the less-developed countries are to grow into the world economy, rather than away from it, they must be encouraged to diversify their exports. Some of them can export a wider range of minerals and crops, but most of them will have to export manufactured goods—textiles, apparel, ceramics, and the like—in order to expand and diversify production. A handful of those countries are already selling manufactured goods in the United States and Western Europe.

In 1964, for example, the developed countries taken together imported $27.3 billion of labor-intensive manufactures, and $2.4 billion, almost 10 per cent, came from the less-developed countries.[7] But center-country tariffs on these manufactured goods are still very high. The average U.S. tariff on textile products is 19 per cent, and its average tariff on ceramic and glass products exceeds 25 per cent (see Table 3-3).[8] These trade barriers, moreover, are apt to rise as the less-developed countries become more competitive. In labor-intensive industries like textiles and apparel, output per man-hour does not differ very much from country to country; a garment worker at a sewing machine is just as efficient in Hong Kong or Bombay as in New York or Milan. Hence, the low-wage, less-developed countries have a distinct cost advantage in labor-intensive production; and when they begin to export manufactures, they sometimes disrupt established markets in the developed countries, forcing workers and communities to make painful adjustments. The center countries are loathe to accept this disruption and have raised new trade barriers, even import quotas, against low-wage textile products. They have promised to liberalize those new trade barriers over a term of years, but their pledge may be more often breached than honored.

If the less-developed countries are to participate more fully in foreign trade, the United States and Western Europe must welcome imports from the periphery—raw materials and manufactures alike. The Trade Expansion Act of 1962 envisaged this possibility, and sought to create an open Atlantic community that would furnish the less-developed countries with growing markets for their young industries. But the Kennedy round of tariff bargaining has gone quite slowly, and no one now expects that tariffs will come down by as much as was envisaged in the Trade Expansion Act. Furthermore, many of the less-developed countries would not be content with easier access to the center countries' markets. They ask, instead, for special treatment, because their new industries cannot yet compete with manufacturers in the developed countries. They call for a *preferential* reduction in tariffs that would not apply to other developed countries. These tariff preferences would breach the basic principle embodied in GATT—the most-favored-nation rule that bars discrimination in tariff policy. But they might be justified if they really served to foster rapid growth and, in particular, caused the less-developed countries to rely less heavily on "import substitution" and infant-industries protection. Too many of the low-income countries have sought to develop by limiting imports and offering protection to high-cost manufacturers who may never outgrow the need for protection.

[7] See Hal B. Lary, "Trade of the LDC's: Manufactures Point the Way," *Columbia Journal of World Business,* Summer, 1966, p. 75.

[8] Contrary to common belief, however, the tariffs of the major industrial countries are not biased against the less-developed countries; they do not afford special protection to the most labor-intensive industries. See Bela Balassa, "Tariff Protection in Industrial Countries: An Evaluation," *Journal of Political Economy,* December, 1965, p. 585.

The United States and Western Europe could also aid development by seeking to stabilize trade in raw materials. The instability of raw-materials prices is costly to the world as a whole because it propels the less-developed countries toward self-sufficiency: as they cannot earn a steady income by selling raw materials, those countries seek to reduce their dependence on center-country exports of manufactures.

Attempts to combat price fluctuations—attempts involving *commodity agreements* to regulate production, trade, or prices—have not been too successful. The international sugar agreement imposed export quotas on the producing countries in order to regulate supply; the international tin agreement set up a *buffer stock* of tin under the management of an International Tin Council, and instructed the Council to buy and sell tin so as to smooth out prices; another agreement covers trade in coffee, and a fourth may be negotiated to regulate the cocoa trade—but none of these agreements has worked very well. It is difficult to penalize the countries that exceed their sugar export quotas, driving prices down. It is hard to know which movements in tin prices should be fought by transactions involving the buffer stock. (At one point, incidentally, the Tin Council ran out of tin and could not keep the price down; in fact, prices soared on word that the stock was low.) And all of these agreements have one major flaw: while working to dampen short-term fluctuations, they also tend to freeze commodity prices, suppressing vital signals of long-run change in world supply and demand. They thereby distort the allocation of resources, much as the American price-support program tends to keep too much labor occupied in agriculture.

For all these reasons, governments are looking for a new approach to stabilization—for ways of compensating low-income countries when their export earnings fall, rather than for ways of manipulating market prices. One such plan is already in operation: in 1963, the International Monetary Fund offered special drawing rights to countries whose export earnings drop below trend. Another, more ambitious plan is still under study. Because IMF drawings must be repaid within a few years they are, in essence, short-term aid and cannot be used to offset a "persistent" short-fall in export earnings. The more ambitious scheme, drafted by the staff of the IBRD, would offer sufficient aid to prevent the disruption of development programs. Each participating country would negotiate a standing agreement with the new international agency managing the scheme. That agreement would contain a projection of the country's export earnings (to be used in identifying subsequent short-falls), and a statement of its foreign-exchange needs, derived from its development plan. When export earnings fell below the projection, a country would first seek assistance from the IMF, and if it needed more, it would turn to the new international agency. Payments by that agency would not be passed on to individual producers, hence would not furnish unwarranted incentives to expand production when prices were falling. They would merely stabilize foreign-exchange receipts, allowing the country to proceed with its planned development, unhampered by balance-of-payments crises. If, later, export earnings rose compared to the export projection, the country would be bound to turn over the "surplus" in repayment of past aid. But if this did not happen (or the "surplus" was too small), the country's net debt to the agency would then be amortized over a long period of years.

Foreign Aid and Investment

If the periphery could count on a stable flow of foreign exchange and a growing market for its manufactured exports, the prospects for development would be enhanced. Yet the low-income countries would still need foreign capital in order to exploit their opportunities. According to one estimate, some $12 billion is needed every year to increase per-capita income by a modest 2 per cent. This is half again as much as the total flow in 1964, described by Table 6-2.

There are ways to stimulate the flow of private capital. For some time, the United States has provided guaranties against the special hazards of foreign investment—expropriation, exchange depreciation, and war damage. Now, it offers "all risk" guaranties. A company that plans to build a plant abroad can buy a guaranty from the U.S. government, to compensate the company if its assets are confiscated, frozen, or destroyed. Several countries give tax incentives to their investors. The United States, for example, permits an American company to defer its U.S. taxes on income earned abroad, and may soon offer an outright tax credit favoring investment in the less-developed countries. German companies can already take a temporary tax deduction when they make a new investment overseas. Finally, the center countries have sought to foster a joint flow of private and official funds. The International Finance Corporation (IFC), a subsidiary of the IBRD, is empowered to invest its funds in new private projects. It can buy non-voting stock in a new enterprise and claim a share in the profits, then can sell off its investment when the project gains momentum and private investors are prepared to commit more capital. In effect, the IFC acts as a catalyst: by investing its own funds, it seeks to encourage a complementary flow of private capital.

The IBRD or World Bank also works to mobilize private capital by selling its own bonds in the developed countries, then making loans to governments and private firms in the less-developed countries. It lays special stress on transport and power, but also finances industrial and agricultural projects. In 1965, the IBRD lent $1 billion to 34 countries, including $134 million to India. In that same year, it borrowed $600 million in Canada, Germany, Switzerland, and the United States. But there are important limits to the work it can do. Because it must pay interest on its own bonds and must redeem them in convertible currencies, it is compelled to charge 5½ per cent or more on its loans to the less-developed countries, and must be repaid in **107** convertible currencies. These terms impose a heavy burden on many borrowers —those whose debt-service payments have grown very large compared to their incomes and export earnings. If, then, there is to be an increased flow of funds to the less-developed countries, there must be more foreign aid and long-term, low-interest public lending.

This news has discouraged many Americans. The United States, after all, has been aiding other countries for a quarter-century. It gave Lend-Lease assistance to its war-time allies, then furnished relief to both victors and vanquished. The Marshall Plan helped to finance post-war reconstruction, and the Mutual Security Program gave arms aid to strengthen the non-communist world against the threat of Soviet aggression. For more than a decade, moreover, the United States has been lending large sums of money to the less-developed countries through the Export-Import Bank and the Agency for International Development; has furnished food and fiber on favorable terms; and has contributed to the United Nations, the IBRD, the Interamerican Development Bank, and the International Development Association, youngest of the IBRD affiliates which makes long-term, low-interest loans to the less-developed countries. In 1964, U.S. aid and lending totalled $3.2 billion, accounting for much more than half of the total public flow to the less-developed countries (see Table 6-2).

Our sacrifice, however, has not been so large. Total U.S. aid in 1964 absorbed less than seven-tenths of 1 per cent of our gross national product (a smaller fraction than the Belgian, French, or British), and claimed less than 5 per cent of total federal revenues. There are, of course, competing claims on our economy and on the federal budget—defense, space exploration, the war on poverty—but foreign aid ought to have rather high priority. It will not win us friends or military allies, nor can we hope that all of it will be spent efficiently. Worst of all, no one can say that aid will guarantee the rapid growth of the less-developed countries. But most authorities agree that those countries cannot grow if they do not have our help, and that the international community cannot survive if the rich grow richer and the poor do not.

Prospects

Progress in human affairs may sometimes occur by the slow accretion of small changes in existing institutions and arrangements, rather than by radical reform. But if the United States and the other industrial countries are to meet the challenge posed by the new nations, they must draw bolder plans and commit a larger part of their vast resources. Nothing we can do will guarantee success. Trade and aid do not assure development, and development does not assure political stability. It may, in fact, usher in a gigantic upheaval in the new nations. But failure to provide opportunities for trade and to furnish much more aid will certainly inhibit growth at the periphery. Stagnation, moreover, will generate frustrations and discontent that can only bring worse sorts of disorder. To strengthen the industrial center and knit together center and periphery may be the most important and difficult tasks to face the United States in the second half of the twentieth century.

Allen, William R., *International Trade Theory: Hume to Ohlin.* (New York: Random House, 1965.) Excerpts from the classics on trade theory, including the chief contributions of Smith, Ricardo, Mill, and Ohlin.

American Economic Association, *Readings in the Theory of International Trade.* (Philadelphia: Blakiston, 1949.) Includes several major contributions to trade theory; see especially Chapters 1, 4, 5, 10-17.

Condliffe, J. B., *The Commerce of Nations.* (New York: W. W. Norton, 1950.) A detailed history of the international economy, stressing the strategic role of Great Britain.

Friedman, Milton, *Essays in Positive Economics.* (Chicago: University of Chicago Press, 1953.) Contains the classic case for flexible exchange rates.

Haberler, Gottfried, *A Survey of International Trade Theory,* and Corden, W. M., *Recent Developments in the Theory of International Trade.* (Princeton: International Finance Section, 1961 and 1965.) Taken together, these two monographs furnish a comprehensive view of modern theory, shorn of mathematics and complicated diagrams.

Hallstein, Walter, *United Europe: Challenge and Opportunity.* (Cambridge: Harvard University Press, 1962.) Lectures by the President of the EEC Commission, explaining the origins, organization, and objectives of the Common Market.

Hawkins, R. G., and Rolfe, S. E., *A Critical Survey of Plans for International Monetary Reform.* (New York: C. J. Devine Institute, New York University, 1965.) A description and comparison of the best-known plans.

Hicks, J. R., *Essays in World Economics.* (London: Oxford University Press, 1959.) Chapter 3 is a brilliant restatement of the case for free trade.

Johnson, H. G., "Trade Preference and Developing Countries," *Lloyds Bank Review,* April, 1966. A rigorous and sceptical review of preferential arrangements to aid the less-developed countries.

Meade, James E., *The Balance of Payments.* (London: Oxford University Press, 1951.) The classic treatise on balance-of-payments adjustment under various exchange-rate regimes.

Mikesell, Raymond F., *Public International Lending for Development*. (New York: Random House, 1966.) A compact survey of the major aid programs and institutions, raising and reviewing the problems that lie ahead.

Nurkse, Ragnar, *International Currency Experience*. (Geneva: League of Nations, 1944.) A description and critique of international monetary policies during the inter-war period—which exerted tremendous influence on post-war planning.

————, *Equilibrium and Growth in the World Economy*. (Cambridge: Harvard University Press, 1961.) My treatment of "center and periphery" owes much to Nurkse's view; see especially Chapters 7 and 11.

Pincus, John, *Economic Aid and International Cost Sharing*. (Baltimore: The Johns Hopkins Press, 1965.) An interesting attempt to measure the "burdens" of foreign aid and international commodity agreements.

Prebisch, Raul, *Towards a New Trade Policy for Development*. (New York: United Nations, 1964.) The Secretary General of UNCTAD reviews the roles of trade and aid in fostering development; an influential and controversial document.

Robinson, Joan, "The Pure Theory of International Trade," *Review of Economic Studies,* Vol. XIV, No. 2 (1946/47). A superb synthesis of trade theories, with special attention to the role of wages.

Triffin, Robert, *Gold and the Dollar Crisis*. (New Haven: Yale University Press, 1960.) A challenging interpretation of recent international monetary history, and Professor Triffin's celebrated plan for reform of the IMF.

Tsiang, S. C., "Fluctuating Exchange Rates in Countries with Relatively Stable Economies," *International Monetary Fund Staff Papers,* Vol. VII, No. 2 (October, 1959). An interesting contrast with Nurkse's critical reading of inter-war experience.

United States Congress, Joint Economic Committee, *Hearings: The United States Balance of Payments*. (Washington, Government Printing Office, 1965.) Testimony by government officials and individual experts concerning the causes and cure of the U.S. deficit.